Relish
NORTH WEST
SECOND HELPING

Original recipes from the region's
finest chefs and restaurants.
Introduction by chef Paul Askew.

First Published 2017
By Relish Publications
Shield Green Farm, Tritlington,
Northumberland, NE61 3DX.

Twitter: @Relish_Cookbook
Facebook: RelishRestaurantGuide
Instagram: Relish_Cookbook
For cookbooks and recipes visit:
www.relishpublications.co.uk
For publishing enquiries visit:
www.relish-publishing.co.uk

ISBN: 978-0-9934678-4-4

Publisher: Duncan L Peters
General Manager: Teresa Peters
Design: Vicki Brown
Copy and Proofing Coordinator: Valerie McLeod
Relish Photography: Andy Richardson, Kevin Gibson,
Nicky Rogerson and Tim Green
Editorial Consultant: Paul Robertson

Printed in Poland on behalf of Latitude Press

Relish
NORTH WEST
SECOND HELPING
Original recipes from the region's
finest chefs and restaurants.
Introduction by chef Paul Askew.

Relish
NORTH EAST
& YORKSHIRE
SECOND HELPING
Original recipes from the North East and
Yorkshire's finest chefs and restaurants.
Introduction by Kenny Atkinson.

Relish
SCOTLAND
THIRD HELPING
Original recipes from the region's finest chefs
and restaurants. Featuring the Michelin starred
chefs of Scotland.

Relish
SOUTH WEST
SECOND HELPING
Original recipes from the South West's
finest chefs and restaurants.
Introduction by chef Nathan Outlaw.

Welcome to this second edition of Relish North West, with a mouthwatering collection of recipes from the region's finest chefs and restaurants. We know you will enjoy cooking your way through the pages of this beautiful guide.

Since starting Relish Publications in 2009, we are privileged to have worked with hundreds of talented and highly acclaimed chefs, some of the biggest names in British food, and now have a national portfolio of over 25 regional, fine-dining guides and bespoke recipe books.

We have circumnavigated the UK in our hunt for the most highly acclaimed eateries, hidden gems and those highly recommended by other top chefs in the UK.

As the proud owner of a Relish cookbook you can also subscribe for a free Relish Rewards Card which entitles members to exclusive offers at some of the featured restaurants, ranging from a bottle of Champagne to free gifts when you dine.

We love to hear from our readers! Why not post your culinary efforts on our Facebook or Instagram pages? And, if you have any questions for the chefs, email our friendly team - marketing@relishpublications.co.uk.

So, next time you're planning to dine in an outstanding restaurant or cook for friends, tantalise your tastebuds with one of our beautiful books, lie back and think of England, Scotland or Wales and enjoy planning your next meal!

Best wishes and bon appétit *Relish* x

004 CONTENTS

006
CONTENTS

Seared Tuna Tataki, Miso Truffle Ponzu Dressing, Mint, Coriander & Spring Onion Salad with Pineapple Dressing - **Page 090**

009
STARTERS

Harefield Premier Beef Fillet, Celeriac Purée, Emmalie Potatoes, Frazzled Pancetta - **Page 212**

011
MAINS

022   Pan Roast Turbot, Charred Carrots, Smoked Aubergine, Crispy Kale, Pesto

032   TFC - Tattenhall Fried Chicken

042   Sirloin & Cured Brisket of Cumbrian Rose Veal, Buttered Cabbage Parcel, Haricot Blanc Purée, Natural Jus

052   Barbecued Beef, Hispi Cabbage, Smoked Shallot Purée

062   Slow Braised Feather Blade, Truffle Chips, Butternut Squash Purée

072   Best End of Spring Lamb, Courgette & Basil Purée

082   Crab Risotto, Radish, Crème Fraîche, Ponzu & Lime Dressing

092   Summer Beef: Confit Brisket, Crispy Ox Cheek, Dandelion & Burdock Glazed Long Rib, Barreled Oxtail, Summer Beans, Sautéed Kidney

102   Hot & Sugar Cured Mackerel, Celeriac, Pink Grapefruit

112   Orange & Fennel Marinated Pork Belly, Carrot Purée, Caramelised Orange

122   Herdwick Hogget, Braised Barley, Parsley Root, Glazed Mushrooms

132   Roast Best End of Lamb, Braised Shoulder, Rosemary Jus, Goat's Cheese Croquette

142   Maple Cured Gammon Ribeye, Crushed New Potatoes, Roast Celeriac, Savoy Cabbage, Beetroot, Rosemary Onion Jus

152   Belted Galloway, Salsify, Bitter Leaves, Miso

162   Loin of Spring Lamb, Masala Sauce, Pea Purée

172   Cumbrian Venison, Pickled Berries, Smoky Tea Infused Potato

182   Yew Tree Farm Hogget Saddle & Belly, Smoked Potato, Baby Beetroot, Pickled Turnip

192   Pollo al Moro

202   Turbot Carpaccio, Grilled Asparagus, Pine Spruce, Rhubarb, Lemon Confit

212   Harefield Premier Beef Fillet, Celeriac Purée, Emmalie Potatoes, Frazzled Pancetta

222   Roast Goosnargh Duck, Beetroot, Orange, Duck Fat Chips

232   Loin & Belly of Spring Lamb

242   Beef Cheek Cooked in Hay, Pickled Beetroot, Onions, Creamed Potato

013
DESSERTS

015
FOREWORD BY PAUL ASKEW

Food evokes memories and stirs passions. The taste, smell and the look of a dish have the unique ability to transport us to a place, a memory, a point in time, from granny's mince beef and onion shortcrust plate pie to mam's homemade broth with pearl barley - food brings people, friends and families together.

The North West is home to some of the most fabulous ingredients, producers and restaurateurs and this book captures the very essence of what makes our region so special with stunning photography and chefs' top tips.

From the simple and straightforward to the more complex dishes to challenge your culinary skills and tantalise your friends and families taste buds, try them, try them all, be proud and above all, enjoy the feeling of making people happy with the food you have prepared.

The idea to bring the region's top producers and chefs together in one book to create this gastronomic masterpiece is to the great credit of the Relish Publications team. It's a unique opportunity for you, the reader, to sample the culinary delights of the region - pick your favourite dish and visit the chef or producer who created it.

Our region is blessed with some truly fantastic producers, ingredients and very talented chefs.

Their hard work, passion and dedication ensures a plentiful supply of vegetables, salads, meat, fish and game that remains the envy of the rest of the UK. Be inspired by the recipes and plentiful supply of quality ingredients.

It is without doubt the quality of the ingredients I work with at The Art School Restaurant and finding the best suppliers and producers in the region that inspires me. Good food is all about the integrity of the ingredients and for me, my job as a chef is to be inspired by their quality and to do things with the ingredients that is innovative but sympathetic and hopefully show them in their best form.

From our coastal waters, to our forests and fields, our climate shapes our people and our food. Enjoy this book and all that it contains.

Please support the independent artisan restaurants and producers in this book. Be an ambassador for the food culture of our great region and share our story with foodies across the country and beyond.

Paul Askew
Chef Patron, The Art School Restaurant

016
60 HOPE STREET

60 Hope Street, Liverpool, L1 9BZ

0151 707 6060
www.60hopestreet.com

Renovated and transformed in 1999 by brothers Colin and Gary Manning, this family owned and run restaurant is a hive of culinary activity. 60 is spread over three floors of a Georgian Grade 2 listed townhouse in an area rich in culture, history and wonderful architecture.

Award-winning for over 18 years, the restaurant thrives on a changing menu of seasonal British produce. Now entering its nineteenth year, 60 Hope Street prides itself on its cuisine and service. Everything on the menu is created with the best quality seasonal produce, all locally sourced with award-winning seafood from Southport, asparagus from Formby, lamb from Elwy Valley and a cheeseboard decorated only with handmade British and Irish cheeses. 60's owners and their team are passionate and committed to providing the best standard of food delivered by an exceptional, unobtrusive level of service. Colin heads the front of house team and writes the extensive 60 wine list, whilst Gary leads the way in the kitchen along with creative design and marketing.

The brothers' business philosophy underlies everything they do. "We started 60 because of our love for our city and our passion for food, especially local produce. We have been able to build strong relationships with small local suppliers and share our interests with our customers," says Colin.

60 offers a traditional, no-fuss approach, classic in style and accommodating to customers' needs. With a large and loyal following, the 60 Supper Club has developed, which enables guests to meet the producer whether that be a local food supplier, wine merchant or brewer.

The brothers own and operate two other restaurants, the Quarter and Host, both in very close proximity to 60 Hope Street.

Hope Street itself has now become a destination in its own right in the city, not only for theatre goers but for foodies and culture vultures alike seeking out the best Liverpool has to offer in this charming, wonderful, eclectic cultural quarter of the city.

Family owned and run since 1999, award-winning 60 Hope Street, housed in a Georgian Grade II listed building in the 'Cultural Quarter', still delivers on its core values of serving modern British food using the finest produce available.

SPRING RABBIT ASSIETTE

SERVES 4

 Sauvignon Blanc Reserve, Marjan Simčič, Goriška Brda (Slovenia)

Ingredients

Rabbit Terrine And Stuffed Saddle

1 whole rabbit (offal removed, jointed into 4 legs and saddle)
vegetable oil (to cover)
100g carrots (peel reserved)
5 cloves garlic (peeled)
3 sprigs thyme
5 white peppercorns
salt and pepper
100g celery
100g Spanish onion
1 sheet gelatine (soaked in cold water)
50ml hot water
20g parsley (chopped)
½ chicken breast
1 egg white
50ml double cream
sushi nori

Goat's Cheese Mousse

200g goat's cheese
100ml double cream
1 tbsp squid ink powder
salt and pepper

Herb Crumb

100g panko breadcrumbs
½ bunch parsley
3 tsp picked thyme
2 sprigs mint
salt (pinch of)

Dill Oil

1 bunch dill
50ml vegetable oil

To Serve

baby carrots (*blanched*)
broad beans (*blanched*, outer shell removed)
breakfast radishes (thinly sliced)
edible viola flowers, baby red basil

rectangular terrine dish

Method

For The Rabbit Terrine (Prepare 24 hours in advance)

Place the legs in a large pan and cover with the vegetable oil. Add the carrot peelings, garlic, thyme, peppercorns and salt. Cook over a low heat (90°C) for 2 hours until the meat is tender and falling off the bone. Leave to cool.

Remove the legs from the pan, drain, scrape the meat from the bones and shred. Set aside.

Brunoise (2mm) the carrot, onion and celery to make a *mirepoix*.

Gently *sauté* the *mirepoix* with 1 tablespoon of vegetable oil until translucent, without colouring. Season with salt and pepper.

To Assemble The Rabbit Terrine

Dissolve the gelatine in the hot water. Mix the liquid with the shredded rabbit leg, parsley and *mirepoix* until evenly coated. Place in a rectangular terrine dish and cover with cling film. Weigh down the terrine and refrigerate overnight.

For The Stuffed Saddle

Dice the rabbit liver into 1cm cubes.

Blitz the chicken breast, egg white and cream until smooth in a blender. Season with salt and pepper. Fold the liver pieces gently into the mousse and transfer to a piping bag. Place the saddle skin-side down and pipe the mixture into the saddle. Roll and wrap tightly with cling film, seal at both ends with string.

Cook the saddle in boiling water for 25 minutes in a large pan, turning after 15 minutes. When cooked through, cool in iced water. When completely cool, remove the cling film and wrap with sushi nori. Wrap in cling film and refrigerate until ready to use.

For The Goat's Cheese Mousse

Blend all the ingredients together in a large mixing bowl until smooth. Place in a container with a lid and refrigerate until set.

For The Herb Crumb

Preheat the oven to 100°C.

Combine all the ingredients in a mixer and pulse until well mixed. Spread onto an oven tray and bake for 10 minutes.

For The Dill Oil

Blanch the dill in boiling water for 10 seconds, remove quickly and place in iced water. Once cooled, remove and squeeze the water out, place in a blender, add the oil and blitz until smooth.

To Serve

Place a slice of terrine and stuffed saddle on each plate. Serve as pictured, finishing with the dill oil.

Chef's Tip

The remaining rabbit bones and offcuts can be used for stock.

PAN ROAST TURBOT, CHARRED CARROTS, SMOKED AUBERGINE, CRISPY KALE, PESTO

SERVES 4

 Barbera del Monferrato, Tacchino, Piedmont (Italy)

Ingredients

Charred Carrots
1 large bunch English carrots (washed, trimmed)

Smoked Aubergine
2 aubergines
olive oil (drizzle of)
3 shallots (chopped)
2 cloves garlic (chopped)
25g miso paste
salt and pepper

Pesto
120g pine nuts
100g basil
50g parsley
50g mint
120g Parmesan
200ml extra virgin olive oil
1 clove garlic (peeled)
salt and pepper

Crispy Kale
120g curly kale (washed, dried)
½ tsp olive oil
salt and pepper

Turbot
4 turbot fillets (skin on)
1 tbsp vegetable oil
salt and pepper

Method

For The Charred Carrots
Peel the carrots if desired. Cook in a pan of boiling water for 10 minutes, drain and pat dry. Before serving, grill the carrots on a high heat for 2-3 minutes each side until well charred.

For The Smoked Aubergine
Using tongs, place the aubergines over an open flame (either a barbecue or over a domestic gas hob) turning until blistered and blackened and the flesh becomes soft. Once cool enough to handle, peel off the skin and place the aubergine flesh in a large bowl.

Fry the shallots and garlic in a little olive oil in a frying pan for 4-5 minutes until translucent. Stir in the miso paste and cook for a further minute. Cool slightly and purée with the aubergine flesh in a blender until smooth. Season with salt and pepper.

For The Pesto
Toast the pine nuts in a dry frying pan until browned. Place the pine nuts in a food processor with all the other ingredients and blend until smooth. Season to taste.

For The Crispy Kale
Preheat the oven to 150°C.

Line 2 baking trays with parchment. Ensure the kale is torn into small, bite size pieces and toss in a large bowl with the olive oil. Season well with salt and pepper.

Spread the kale over the trays in a single layer. Bake for 18-20 minutes until crisp but still green. Remove it from the oven and leave to cool.

> **Chef's Tip**
> Be careful not to overcook the kale as it will turn brown and bitter.

For The Turbot
Heat the vegetable oil in a non-stick frying pan over a medium/high heat.

Season the turbot on both sides and once the pan is hot, add the turbot fillets skin-side down and cook for 3 minutes until the skin is golden and crisp. Turn the turbot over and cook for a further 2 minutes before taking the pan off the heat, allowing the fish to finish cooking in the hot pan. Check that the fish is cooked all the way through by inserting a metal skewer in the thickest part which will be warm to touch. Serve immediately.

To Serve
Place the turbot golden-side up on a warmed plate. Arrange the charred carrots, a *quenelle* of the smoked aubergine, scatter the crispy kale and drizzle with the pesto.

LEMON & LIME MERINGUE

SERVES 4

 Château Loupiac Gaudiet, Bordeaux (France)

Ingredients

Lemon Curd

4 lemons (juice of)
110g caster sugar
100g unsalted butter
4 large free-range eggs

Lime Curd

5 limes (juice of, zest of 1)
4 large free-range eggs
110g caster sugar
110g unsalted butter

Meringue Kisses

100g egg whites
100g caster sugar
100g icing sugar

Shortbread

250g unsalted butter
110g caster sugar
330g plain flour

Lemon Sponge

100g unsalted butter
100g caster sugar
2 large free-range eggs
100g ground almonds
1 lemon (juice and zest of)

Chantilly Cream

300ml double cream
1 tbsp caster sugar
1 tsp vanilla extract (or ½ tsp vanilla bean paste)

Yoghurt Sorbet

1 litre stock syrup
1 litre natural yoghurt
100ml water
50ml elderflower cordial

Garnish

lemon zest, lime zest
lemon balm

2 baking trays (lined), 2 small cake tins

Method

For The Lemon Curd

Put the lemon juice, sugar and butter into a *bain-marie*. Stir the mixture every now and again until all of the butter has melted. Whisk the eggs, then stir into the lemon mixture until well combined. Leave to cook for 10-12 minutes, stirring occasionally, until the mixture coats the back of a spoon. Remove from the heat and cool. Pour into sterilised jars and seal. Keep in the fridge until ready to use.

For The Lime Curd

Use the same method as for the lemon curd but before storing, stir the lime zest gently into the curd.

For The Meringue Kisses

Preheat the oven to 100°C.
Lightly whip the egg whites in a large bowl adding a little sugar at a time to form soft peaks. Slowly add the icing sugar until smooth and glossy. Scrape the meringue into a large piping bag and pipe approximately 30-40 kisses onto 2 baking trays. Bake for 2 hours, remove from oven and allow to cool.

For The Shortbread

Preheat the oven to 150°C.
Cream the butter and sugar in a large mixing bowl until pale and creamy, then gently mix in the flour, being careful not to overwork the dough. Using your hand, roll the dough into a large ball, place between 2 sheets of greaseproof paper and roll out to the thickness of a pound coin. Refrigerate for 20 minutes until set, then cut into biscuit shapes and bake for 30-40 minutes until pale golden brown. Remove from the oven and cool on a wire rack.

For The Lemon Sponge

Preheat the oven to 180°C.
Cream the butter and sugar in a large mixing bowl until pale and creamy. Add the eggs, one at a time, then fold in the ground almonds and lemon zest. Add lemon juice to give a dropping consistency. Divide between the cake tins and bake for 12-15 minutes until pale golden and springy to touch. Remove and allow to cool for 8 minutes in the tins, then turn out onto wire racks. Once cooled, use mini cookie cutters or cut into desired shapes.

For The Chantilly Cream

Whip the cream, sugar and vanilla together in a large mixing bowl until soft peaks form. Refrigerate until ready to serve.

For The Yoghurt Sorbet

Mix all the ingredients together and churn in an ice cream machine for about 15-20 minutes, or until softly set. Transfer to a container and freeze.

To Serve

Crush some of the meringue kisses and sit the sorbet on top. Assemble as pictured and dress with lemon and lime zest and lemon balm leaves.

026
ALLIUM
BY MARK ELLIS

Lynedale House, High Street, Tattenhall, CH3 9PX

01829 771 477
www.theallium.co.uk Twitter: @AlliumbyMark Facebook: @AlliumRestaurantandBar

Allium is a restaurant and bar with rooms in the picturesque village of Tattenhall in the heart of the Cheshire countryside. The brainchild of acclaimed chef Mark Ellis, Allium is an expression of Mark's background, culinary experience and aspirations for how a restaurant and bar should be experienced.

After learning his trade in some of the best kitchens in the country from Chester to London, Mark returned home to the North West nine years ago to head up the kitchens of the award-winning Peckforton Castle in Tarporley where he quickly earned 3 AA Rosettes amongst numerous other national and local accolades and made two appearances on BBC's The Great British Menu until he left to open his first solo venture, Allium, to outstanding critical acclaim.

Taking the very best of seasonal produce, Allium produces a menu of thought provoking dishes with roots in comfort food from Mark's childhood and his interest in the science of cookery. While the dishes often have playful names, they demonstrate Mark's clever tongue-in-cheek humour and lend a sense of fun to his food, something Mark feels is greatly overlooked in kitchens today. The dishes use a blend of modern, cutting edge techniques mixed with classic, old school processes to produce an outstanding plate of food that is as beautiful as it is delicious. Customers can choose individual dishes from the main menu, or opt for Mark's signature seven-course 'Experience' menu, which has proved to be a huge hit with diners, as have the little touches that make Allium a truly unique fine dining venue, such as live music at the weekend and a close up magician performing to diners at their table.

Allium truly is Cheshire's jewel in the crown and a magical experience not to be missed.

Allium

[al-ee-uh m] noun

1. any bulbous plant belonging to the genus Allium, of the amaryllis family, having an onion odour and flower in a round cluster, including the onion, leek, shallot, garlic, and chive.

2. a modern Restaurant and Room with Rooms that

CHOUCROUTE - SEA TROUT, BLACK TREACLE, FENNEL

SERVES 4

 We pair this with a perfect serve Dà Mhile seaweed gin and tonic!

Ingredients

Choucroute

1 head fennel (washed, dried well)
200g salt
sparkling water (to rinse)
100g caster sugar
100ml Chardonnay vinegar
100ml still water
100ml white wine
1 bay leaf
1 sprig fresh thyme
6 white peppercorns
1 star anise
30g chives (finely sliced)

Cured Sea Trout

1kg side fresh sea trout (skinned and pin boned)
750g rock salt
500g sugar
500g black treacle
20g orange zest
10 white peppercorns
250ml water

Sea Trout Confit

500g fresh sea trout (scaled, pin boned)
rapeseed oil (to drizzle)
salt
2 sprigs thyme

Fennel Pollen

200g fennel tops and stalks (chopped)
100g fennel seeds (lightly toasted)
100g dill
100g bronze fennel herb
2 star anise (toasted)
50g tarragon
50g bee pollen
1 lemon (zest of)

Method

For The Choucroute (Prepare ahead)

Pick the green tops off the fennel and remove the stalks. Reserve for the pollen. Cut the bulb in half and cut out the tough centre. Using a mandoline, finely slice the fennel and lay on a tray in an even layer. Sprinkle evenly with salt, cover and leave for 2 hours. Wash off the salt with sparkling water and dry. Bring the sugar, vinegar, water, wine, bay, thyme, peppercorns and star anise to the boil. Remove from the heat and cool.

Mix the pickle and fennel and vac pack a couple of times to instantly infuse the fennel. Alternatively, mix together and leave for 24 hours.

For The Cured Sea Trout (Allow 48 hours)

Mix the salt, sugar, 250g of the treacle, orange zest, and peppercorns in a blender until well combined. Roll out a layer of cling film and spoon on half of the salt mixture, then place the sea trout on top. Cover the fish with the remaining salt, then draw the sides of the cling film together to make a parcel, ensuring that the fish is fully and evenly coated in the mixture. Transfer to a tray and refrigerate for 24 hours. Remove the cling film and wash off the salt mixture under running water. Mix the remaining treacle with the water to make a paste, pour into a tray and sit the fish on top (this will stain the fish black and further infuse the treacle flavour). Store overnight in the fridge.

For The Sea Trout Confit

Cut the sea trout into 4 even slices against the grain of the flesh. Coat in the rapeseed oil and season well. Place into a vac pack bag with the thyme and seal. Cook in a 45°C water bath for 30 minutes. Remove just before serving. Alternatively, gently steam.

For The Fennel Pollen (Prepare ahead)

Finely chop all the ingredients and dehydrate in the oven for 12 hours (50°C fan) whilst retaining a green colour. Blend to a powder in a spice grinder.

To Assemble The Dish

Mix the choucroute with the chives and plate. Finely slice the cured fish against the grain and roll the slices into roses. Remove the cooked fish from the vac pack bag and pat dry with kitchen paper. Slice the fish into 2 pieces and blow torch the skin to crisp up. Garnish with bronze leaf fennel, a pinch of the fennel pollen and some dots of treacle.

Chef's Tip

Fennel can be treated just like a hard cabbage; perfect for pickling or fermenting. A mandoline is essential to slice finely and evenly.

TFC - TATTENHALL FRIED CHICKEN

SERVES 4

 Combe Aux Jacques Beaujolais-Villages (France)

Ingredients

Spice Mix (Combine all ingredients well)

400g dried mixed herbs, 100g garlic powder
100g Himalayan pink salt, 20g dried chilli powder
100g cracked black pepper, 100g paprika
2 chicken stock cubes

Chicken Legs

50g table salt, 500ml water
4 large free-range chicken legs
500g duck fat, 1 sprig thyme, 2 bay leaves
6 white peppercorns
25g transglutaminase
2 eggs, 500ml buttermilk, 500g spice mix
300g plain flour, oil (to deep fry)

Chicken Breasts

2 chicken breasts (skin removed and reserved for the crisps)
25g *rendered* chicken fat
100g spice mix

Sweetcorn Purée

400g sweetcorn kernels, 20g shallots (minced)
½ saffron, 80g potato (finely diced), 20g butter
500ml vegetable *nage*, 200ml whipping cream
3g xanthan gum, 20ml corn oil

Charred Kernels

20g butter, 1 ear fresh corn on the cob

Chicken Gravy

2½ litres fresh chicken stock
3 carrots (chopped, browned)
1 stick celery (chopped)
1 onion (halved, blackened on each cut side)
1 leek (sliced), ½ bulb garlic (halved)
4 pigs trotters (roasted, or 5 sheets gelatine)
4 sprigs thyme, 4 sprigs rosemary
arrowroot (dispersed with water, as required)

Chicken Crisps

100g chicken skin, 50g *clarified butter*
pink Himalayan salt (to sprinkle)

Method

For The Chicken Legs (Allow 24 hours)

Mix the water and salt and chill for 1 hour. Place the legs in the brine and chill for 1 hour. Remove the legs and rinse well (reserve the brine for the chicken breasts). Vac pack the legs with the duck fat, thyme, bay and peppercorns and cook for 90 minutes at 72°C. Alternatively, place the legs in a deep tray with the aromats and cover with melted duck fat. Cook at 140°C (fan) for 2 hours. Cool the legs and flake off all the meat. Evenly lay the meat onto a tray and, using a fine tea strainer, coat the chicken with the transglutaminase. Lay the chicken on a double layer of cling film and roll into a tight cylinder. Refrigerate overnight.

When ready to serve, mix the eggs with the buttermilk. Remove the cling film from the chicken and coat well in the buttermilk mixture. Mix the spice mix with the flour and coat the chicken well. Deep fry at 180°C until crisp and golden.

For The Chicken Breasts

Trim any fat from the breasts and soak in the reserved brine for 1 hour in the fridge. Rinse well. Rub the chicken fat all over the breast and repeat with the spice mix. Vac pack and cook in a water bath for 1 hour at 60°C. Alternatively, lightly poach or steam until just cooked, about 20 minutes.

For The Sweetcorn Purée

Sweat the sweetcorn with the shallot, saffron and potato in butter. Add the vegetable *nage* and simmer until evaporated. Add the cream and reduce by a third. Pour into a blender with the xanthan gum and corn oil and blend on full speed until smooth and glossy. Pass through a sieve and check the seasoning.

For The Charred Kernels

Soften the butter and rub all over the corn. Season and char on a grill. Allow to cool and with a sharp knife, cut down against the grain to release the individual kernels.

For The Chicken Gravy

Add all the ingredients, except the arrowroot, to a large pan and simmer gently. Reduce the stock until the desired strength of flavour is achieved. Use a little arrowroot to thicken the gravy, then simmer for 5-10 minutes.

For The Chicken Crisps

Preheat the oven to 160°C (fan).

With a sharp knife, scrape the inside of the chicken skin to remove the excess fat. Place the skin on a heavy, flat tray lined with silicone paper. Brush with the *clarified butter*, then top with a piece of silicone paper and another heavy tray and bake for 15-20 minutes or until crispy. Remove from the tray and cool on a wire rack. Season with pink Himalayan salt.

To Assemble The Dish

Lightly char the chicken breasts on a grill then slice in half through the middle. Top the breast with the crispy skin. Add the other elements to the plate and finish with the gravy.

CARIBBEAN - COCONUT PARFAIT, LIME, CARDAMOM, RUM, VANILLA

SERVES 4

 Havana Club 7 year old rum, served over ice

Ingredients

Coconut Parfait

375g egg yolk
160g caster sugar
750g coconut purée
28g gelatine (softened in cold water)
900ml whipping cream (whipped)
300g desiccated coconut (toasted)

Ice Cream

875ml whole milk
250ml double cream
5g fresh mint
30 cardamom pods
220g caster sugar
10 pasteurised egg yolks
2 limes (microplaned zest of)

Vanilla Curd

270ml double cream
3g agar agar
270g egg yolks
180g caster sugar
270g butter (melted)
2 vanilla pods (split)

Rum Glass

500g caster sugar
500ml water
1 lemon (zest of)
1 vanilla pod (split, scraped)
50ml Mount Gay rum
6 leaves gelatine (soaked in cold water)

Garnish (optional)

gold leaf
dehydrated lime zest

Method

For The Coconut Parfait

In a *bain-marie*, *sabayon* the eggs and the sugar. Add the coconut purée and cook to 83°C, whisking constantly. Add the gelatine and whisk until dissolved. Cool the mixture to room temperature and fold in the whipped cream in 3 stages. Using cling film, roll into a cylinder shape and freeze. When solid, remove from the freezer and remove the cling film. Using a blow torch, gently heat the outside of the parfait, then transfer to a tray with the toasted coconut and roll the parfait until well coated. Keep in the fridge until required.

For The Ice Cream

Bring the milk, cream, mint and cardamom to the boil. Remove from the heat and infuse for 1 hour, then strain. Whisk the yolks and sugar until pale, then *temper* the yolks with a third of the cream mix. Add back to the pan with the rest of the cream mixture and gently heat to 81°C, constantly stirring. Remove from the heat and blend for 1 minute. Pass through a sieve and cool the mixture. Add the lime and blend again before churning in an ice cream machine. Store in a freezer until needed.

For The Vanilla Curd

Bring the cream, vanilla pods and agar agar to the boil in a heavy-based pan.

Mix the yolks and sugar, then pour over the cream and mix well. Return the cream and egg mixture to a pan and cook over a low heat until the eggs are almost scrambled. Remove the vanilla and blend at high speed in a food processor, slowly adding the butter until a thick, shiny *emulsion* is formed. Pass the mixture through a fine *chinois* into a squeezy bottle and chill.

For The Rum Glass (Prepare ahead)

Combine the sugar, water, lemon and vanilla in a pan and bring to the boil. Reduce the heat and simmer gently for 10 minutes. Add the gelatine and stir well. Remove from the heat and pass through a fine sieve into a container. Add the rum and cool to room temperature before setting in the fridge for 12 hours. Remove from the container and chop until the gel resembles fine glass (work quickly so the gel does not melt.) Carefully spoon the rum glass onto a tray lined with silicone paper and freeze for 30 minutes.

To Assemble The Dish

Swipe some vanilla curd across the plate and arrange the rum glass next to it. Add the parfait and dot the vanilla curd. Finish with a ball of ice cream. At the restaurant, we garnish with gold leaf and dehydrated lime zest.

THE ART SCHOOL RESTAURANT

1 Sugnall Street, Liverpool, L7 7EB

0151 230 8600
www.theartschoolrestaurant.co.uk Twitter: @ArtSchoolLpool
Facebook: The Art School Restaurant Liverpool

The Art School is a 50 cover fine dining restaurant situated in the heart of Liverpool's Georgian Quarter. Critically acclaimed, the restaurant offers a range of pescatarian, vegetarian and vegan menus alongside its pre-theatre, Excellence and Tasting menus.

Using only the finest ingredients from local suppliers, the experienced team of home grown and international chefs, waiters and sommeliers deliver the highest quality service in a relaxed setting.

The seasonal menus are perfectly matched with an exclusive range of organic spirits, a 280-bin wine list and a world class selection of Champagnes. The restaurant was recently named in the Sunday Times Top 100 Restaurants for 2017 and is winner of the Visit England Excellence Awards Taste category 2017. Chef patron Paul Askew is committed to developing local talent and was responsible for the Royal Academy of Culinary Arts qualification coming to the region in 2016. Paul has featured on Saturday Morning Kitchen and the Great British Menu, where his main course dish scored 'the perfect 10'.

"The finest seasonal ingredients treated with care, attention and respect, with a simple approach of what grows together goes together". The culinary philosophy of chef patron Paul Askew.

FILLET OF RED MULLET, BLOOD ORANGE DRESSING, HERB INFUSED GOAT'S CURD CHEESE, NASTURTIUM, GOLDEN BEETS

SERVES 4

Lagar De Bouza, Albariño, Rias, (Spain)
Fabulous acidity and citrus fruits contrasting with
the savoury, salty notes of the red mullet and
goat's curd.

Ingredients

Beetroot

2 golden beetroots (peeled, cut into 1cm dice)
½ litre vegetable stock
saffron (pinch of)
Maldon salt (to taste)
caster sugar (to taste)

Herb Infused Goat's Curd Cheese

½ lemon (zest of)
25g chives (chopped)
freshly ground white pepper and salt (to taste)
50g Curthwaite goat's curd

Blood Orange Dressing

1 tbsp wholegrain mustard
½ banana shallot (finely diced)
cider vinegar (splash of)
2 blood oranges (peeled, segmented, juice reserved)
10ml extra virgin olive oil

Salad

frisee (handful of)
watercress (handful of)
nasturtium (handful of)
1 red onion (finely sliced)
salt and freshly ground white pepper (to taste)

Red Mullet

4 x 100g red mullet fillets
1 tbsp vegetable oil
salt (pinch of)
Espelette powder (dusting of)
½ lemon (juice of)

Method

For The Beetroot

Cook the beetroots in the stock with the saffron, salt and sugar until cooked and the stock reduced. Allow to cool and keep refrigerated in the cooking *liquor.*

For The Herb Infused Goat's Curd Cheese

Mix the lemon zest, white pepper and salt with the chopped chives and goat's curd. Transfer to a piping bag and refrigerate until needed.

For The Blood Orange Dressing

Mix the mustard with the shallot, vinegar and the juice of the blood oranges. *Emulsify* with the olive oil and adjust the seasoning before adding the blood orange segments.

For The Salad

Wash and pick the frisee, watercress and nasturtium leaves. Add to a bowl with the onion and mix with a little of the blood orange dressing. Season just prior to plating up.

For The Red Mullet

Place the fillets, skin-side down, on a sheet of silicone paper which has been oiled and lightly salted. Season the fish flesh with a little salt and Espelette powder. Grill for 2-3 minutes. Finish with a squeeze of lemon and serve skin-side up.

To Serve

Plate as pictured and enjoy.

> **Chef's Tip**
>
> Use the Espelette powder to season the mullet before grilling. Ask your fishmonger to descale, fillet and pin bone for you to save some time and make sure you use the head and bones for a great fish stock.

SIRLOIN & CURED BRISKET OF CUMBRIAN ROSE VEAL, BUTTERED CABBAGE PARCEL, HARICOT BLANC PUREE, NATURAL JUS

SERVES 4

 Vallet Frères, Gevrey Chambertin 'Clos de la Justice' Burgundy Pinot Noir (France)

Ingredients

Veal Stock And Rose Veal Jus

reserved veal bones (from the veal sirloin)
mirepoix (2 carrots, 2 leeks, 2 stick celery, chopped)
2 bay leaves, 6 peppercorns
5 litres water, 25g cold butter (diced)

Cured Rose Veal Brisket

300-400g piece rose veal brisket, 100g salt
100g sugar, 1 tsp fennel seeds, ⅔ veal stock

Haricot Bean Purée

500g dried haricot blanc beans (soaked overnight)
salt (pinch of), ½ onion, 4 cloves garlic
1 large potato (peeled), white pepper (to taste)
Maldon sea salt (to taste)
olive oil or unsalted butter (knob of)

Cabbage Parcels

½ Savoy or Hispi cabbage (sliced)
50g butter (plus extra for grilling)
1 shallot (diced), 1 clove garlic (chopped)
1 sprig thyme (picked), salt and pepper
50g Parmesan, double cream (splash of)
4 spring cabbage outer leaves

Charred Leek Powder

3 large leeks (cleaned), 3 cloves black garlic
10g black garlic salt, 70g caster sugar

Rose Veal Sirloin

4 x 120g rose veal sirloin medallions (trimmed,
bones removed and reserved, seasoned)
Maldon salt and freshly milled pepper (to season)
2 sprigs thyme, 1 tbsp sunflower or vegetable oil
butter (large knob of)

To Serve

4 baby heritage carrots (peeled, *blanched*)
4 baby leeks (cleaned, *blanched*, refreshed)
salsify (*blanched*, *sautéed*), fresh chervil sprigs

Method

For The Veal Stock And Rose Veal Jus (Prepare ahead)

Preheat the oven to 180°C.

Roast the bones for 45 minutes in the oven. Add the vegetables, cover in water and simmer for 4½ hours. Pass through muslin and portion into 3. Prior to serving, reduce one third of the stock to a syrup and whisk in the cold butter to create a smooth jus.

For The Cured Rose Veal Brisket (Allow 48 hours)

Rub the brisket with the cure ingredients and refrigerate overnight.

Wash off the cure and braise in one portion of the stock until tender, about 2 hours. Press and refrigerate overnight. Discard the liquid.

Preheat the oven to 160°C.

Seal the brisket in a hot, heavy-based roasting tray. Add the last stock portion to the tray and roast for 3½ hours until tender.

For The Haricot Bean Purée (Prepare ahead)

Rinse the beans and cook in salted water with garlic and vegetables until soft, about 25-30 minutes. Remove the garlic and vegetables, then blitz the beans to a smooth purée. Season, then add butter or oil to finish.

For The Cabbage Parcels (Prepare the day before)

Sweat the sliced cabbage, shallot, butter, garlic, thyme and seasoning in a pan without browning. Allow to cool a little before adding the Parmesan and a splash of cream. Mix well and chill overnight.

Blanch and de-vein the spring cabbage leaves. Dry well. Roll the chilled mixture tightly in the cabbage leaves, then wrap in cling film. Chill until required. Remove the cling film, slice and reheat to serve by steaming, or brush with melted butter and grill.

For The Charred Leek Powder

Preheat the oven to 200°C.

Dry roast the leeks and black garlic for 30 minutes or until black. Cool, then blitz to a fine powder with the garlic salt and sugar.

For The Rose Veal Sirloin

Season the veal, then seal in a hot pan with a drizzle of oil and the thyme for 1 minute on each side. Add the butter and baste for a further minute on each side (medium rare is best), then allow to rest for 6-8 minutes before carving.

To Serve

Garnish with chervil and serve as pictured.

PEANUT BUTTER & CHOCOLATE BROWNIE, CHOCOLATE ICE CREAM, RASPBERRY COULIS

SERVES 8

🍷 *Ben Ryé Dessert Wine, Donnafugata (Sicily)*

Ingredients

Peanut Butter And Chocolate Brownie

113g smooth peanut butter
43g icing sugar
72g coconut oil
1½ vanilla pods (scraped)
salt (pinch of)
85g dark chocolate (70% solids)
76ml soya milk
½ tbsp cornflour
85g caster sugar
96g ground almonds
3 tbsp cocoa powder
½ tsp baking powder

Chocolate Ice Cream

565ml whole milk
160ml double cream
75-100ml Rhodda's clotted cream
50g skimmed milk powder
40g dextrose
60g egg yolk
125g sugar
75g Valrhona chocolate

Raspberry Coulis

200g raspberry purée, 2g agar agar

Popcorn

popcorn kernels (handful of)
oil (drizzle of), salt (pinch of)

Candied Nuts

25g butter, 25g caster sugar
50g peanuts

Garnish

edible flowers

25cm x 20cm x 5cm baking tin (greased, lined)

Method

For The Peanut Butter And Chocolate Brownie

Preheat the oven to 160°C.

Combine the peanut butter, icing sugar, 1 tablespoon of the coconut oil, one third of the vanilla seeds and salt and mix until smooth.

Melt the chocolate with the remaining coconut oil in a *bain-marie*.

Whisk together the milk, remaining vanilla seeds and the cornflour, then add in the warm chocolate and mix well. Stir in the sugar, then sift in the almonds, cocoa powder and baking powder.

Pour the chocolate batter into the prepared tin and drop spoonfuls of the peanut butter mix on top and swirl. Bake for 17 minutes.

For The Chocolate Ice Cream

Pour the milk, creams, milk powder and dextrose into a saucepan and bring to the boil.

Beat the egg yolks with the sugar in a bowl, then pour the hot cream over. Continue to beat until everything is combined. Pour the mixture back into the pan and cook on a low heat for 3-4 minutes, stirring continuously until the consistency of thin custard. Remove from the heat. Stir in the chocolate until melted, then chill. Churn in an ice cream machine until frozen.

> **Chef's Tip**
> Prepare the ice cream and brownie the day before. You can gently reheat the brownie in the oven for 5 minutes to achieve a soft, gooey texture.

For The Raspberry Coulis

Heat the purée until boiling, then whisk in the agar agar. Allow to cool. Refrigerate until firm, then blitz to a gel-like paste.

For The Popcorn

Heat the oil and kernels in a heavy-based pan with a lid on until the kernels stop popping. Remove from the heat and sprinkle with salt.

For The Candied Nuts

Melt the butter and sugar together in a heavy-based pan until it begins to caramelise. Toss in the peanuts, then leave to cool on a silicone mat.

To Serve

Serve as pictured.

046
ASKHAM HALL

Askham, Penrith, Cumbria, CA10 2PF

01931 712 350
www.askhamhall.co.uk Twitter: @AskhamHall Facebook: Askham Hall

A stunning Grade 1 listed Pele Tower dating back to the late 1200s, Askham Hall has recently been transformed from a stately family home into a unique and contemporary stylish retreat and restaurant. Set in the unspoilt Eden Valley on the edge of the Lake District, a luxurious, intimate, unpretentious home from home awaits.

With modern furnishings and fresh décor, whilst carefully retaining the charm and character of this historic house, Askham Hall is somewhere you can relax in down to earth, comfortable surroundings. The antithesis of the traditional country house hotel, it is a bohemian-style retreat with a wonderful vegetable patch, fields and ponds with animals, set in the heart of an incredibly productive area for wild food.

The beautifully remodelled dining area is made up of three exquisite rooms and overseen by renowned chef Richard Swale, offering a unique and creative dining style using produce sourced from the surrounding fields and gardens and the 800-year-old family estate. Private dining for various group sizes is also available in the original oak panelled dining room or the recently refurbished medieval hall.

The cycle of life in the gardens and fields dictates the menus - they work with the seasons to grow, source and preserve the produce from the farms and woodlands. The gardens are tended by Colin Myers who ensures an abundance of fresh, seasonal produce and completing the team is owner Charles Lowther, with his passion for livestock including Shorthorn cattle.

Continuing on from the success of their nearby sister establishment, the award-winning George and Dragon, Askham Hall promises a stunning menu, having featured in Taste Cumbria (Cumbria Tourism) 2015 and secured a new entry in the Good Food Guide 2017.

Richard Swale grew up in Cumbria. He trained with John Burton Race and Anthony Demetre, before working in France. Richard has also undertaken placements around Europe which include Marc Veyrat and Noma.

CARPACCIO OF SCALLOPS, ELDERFLOWER, CELERIAC, APPLE, WALNUTS

SERVES 4

Sancerre, Les Caillottes, Pascal Jolivet, Loire, 2015 (France)
Jolivet is of the dynamic, outward looking, highly qualified new generation of French winemakers combining modern techniques with their unbeatable raw product to end up with world class wine. A dazzling Sancerre, razor sharp and lingering. This wine is a perfect match to this starter with its own notes of elderflower and mineral complexity.

Ingredients

Pickled Celeriac

25g caster sugar
75ml white wine vinegar
125ml water
200g celeriac (diced into ½cm cubes)

Celeriac Purée

300g celeriac (finely chopped)
butter (large knob of)
100ml double cream
50ml whole milk
lemon juice (spritz of)
salt (pinch of)

Apple Purée

3 Granny Smith apples (peeled, diced)
butter (knob of)
sugar (pinch of)
water (dash of)

Carpaccio Of Scallops

12 large scallops (raw)
50ml elderflower vinegar (white wine vinegar infused with elderflower)
100ml olive oil
sea salt (pinch of)

To Serve

apple (cut into sticks)
mini watercress
walnuts (chopped)

Method

For The Pickled Celeriac

Bring the sugar, vinegar and water to the boil in a pan. Add the celeriac and cook until *al dente*, about 1 minute. Leave to cool in the liquid.

For The Celeriac Purée

Sweat the celeriac in the butter for around 5 minutes. Do not allow it to colour or burn. Add the cream and milk and cook slowly until you have a thick, lumpy purée. Transfer to a blender and blitz to a smooth purée. Season with salt and lemon juice. Place in a squeezy bottle and set aside.

For The Apple Purée

Sweat the chopped apple in a knob of butter, with a pinch of sugar and a little water. Cook until soft, then blend until smooth. Transfer into a squeezy bottle and set aside.

For The Carpaccio Of Scallops

Thinly slice the raw scallops and layer on a serving plate. Mix the oil and elderflower vinegar and brush over the scallops. Season each slice of scallop with sea salt.

To Serve

Neatly dot the celeriac and apple purées around the scallop carpaccio. Evenly place the pickled celeriac around the plate, along with the apple sticks, walnuts and watercress.

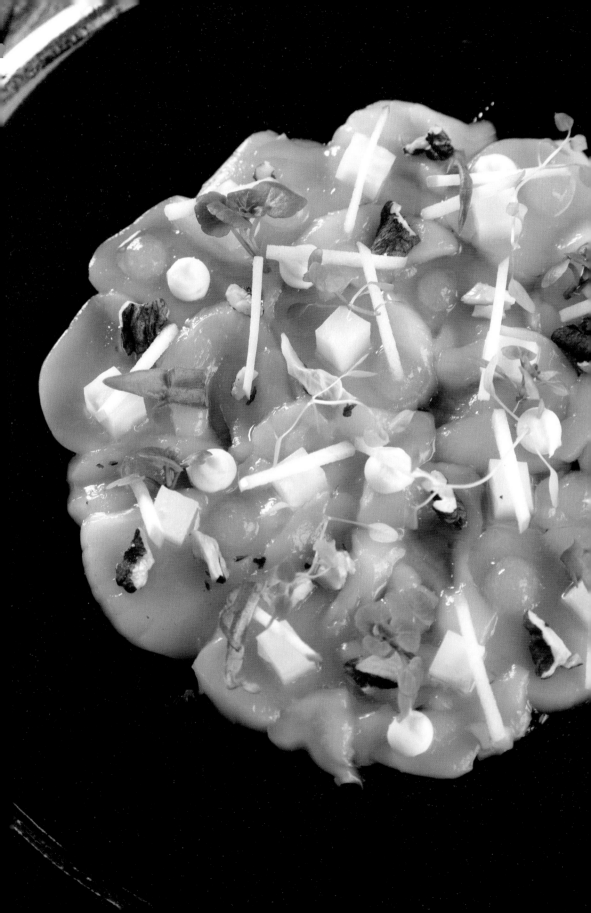

BARBECUED BEEF, HISPI CABBAGE, SMOKED SHALLOT PUREE

SERVES 4

Zorzal Eggo, Tupungato, Mendoza, 2012 (Argentina)
Termed a field blend, this intense and vital red is made up from mostly Malbec with whatever else is ripe at the harvest. Fermented in egg shaped concrete vats, hence the name, this tangy red has no oak ageing. Juicy, with firm structure and a distinctive, lively finish. Traditionally Malbec and beef work in perfect harmony and the juicy fruit of this example offers a sumptuous reward when eaten with our own Shorthorn beef.

Ingredients

4 flat iron bavette steaks

Green Sauce

6g unsalted butter
10g parsley
10g tarragon
5g salted anchovies
5g Dijon mustard
4ml lemon juice
1 small clove garlic
salt and pepper

Smoked Shallot Purée

200g banana shallots (peeled, sliced)
butter (knob of)
100ml double cream

Beef Sauce

200g shallots (sliced)
butter (knob of)
200g button mushrooms (sliced)
1 sprig thyme
1 bay leaf
400ml Madeira
1 litre fresh beef stock

To Serve

roasted baby onions
hispi cabbage (wilted)
bowl of chips

Method

For The Green Sauce

Melt the butter and place all the ingredients into a blender. Blend to a smooth sauce, season to taste.

For The Smoked Shallot Purée

Caramelise the shallots in a pan with the butter until they are totally brown. If you have a barbecue with a lid, light the barbecue and add some smoking chips - this is optional. Place the shallots onto a tray and smoke for 5 minutes. Return the shallots to the pan and add the cream. Cook down until thick, then blend and set aside.

For The Beef Sauce

Caramelise the shallots in a knob of butter. Add the mushrooms, thyme and bay leaf and cook for a further 2 minutes. Add the Madeira and reduce by half, then add the stock and cook for 30 minutes. Pass the liquid through a fine sieve and discard the solids. Reduce the liquid down until a sauce consistency.

Piecing It Together

Grill or barbecue the steaks to your preference. Warm the shallot purée, beef sauce and green sauce. Slice the steaks and arrange with the cabbage and onions. Finish with the different sauces and serve with a side of chips.

Chef's Tip

Add smoked salt to the beef for a more barbecue flavour.

PARSNIP RICE PUDDING, SPICED PLUMS

SERVES 4

Gewurztraminer Selection Grains Nobles Cuvée Anne, Domaine Schlumberger, Alsace, 2009 (France)
Elegant and expressive wine made from late harvested grapes. Deep gold in colour, the wine displays sublime candied orange as well as roasted pineapple and papaya. A rare and delicious wine from the finest vineyards in Alsace. Rice pudding is a classic dish in Alsatian cuisine so naturally it's only fitting to pair it with this nectar.

Ingredients

Parsnip Rice Pudding

500g parsnips (peeled, diced to 1cm cubes)
butter (knob of)
1 litre semi-skimmed milk
½ vanilla pod
250g pudding rice
1 tsp mixed spice
nutmeg (pinch of)
75g sugar
300ml double cream
¼ lemon (zest of)
¼ orange (zest of)

Spiced Plums

300ml red wine
150ml port
200ml fresh orange juice
5 cloves
1 star anise
½ stick cinnamon
125g sugar
750g plums (halved, stones removed)

Parsnip Crisps

1 large parsnip (peeled)
freeze-dried blackberry powder (optional)

Garnish

basil leaves

Method

For The Parsnip Rice Pudding

Sweat the parsnips in a little butter for 2 minutes, then add the milk and vanilla pod and bring to a simmer for about 25 minutes. Set aside for about 1 hour, then pass through a sieve and save.

Pour 700ml of the infused milk into a large pan and add the pudding rice and spices. Simmer for 15-20 minutes until the liquid is absorbed. Once cooked, add the sugar and cream and cook for a further 5 minutes. Set aside.

For The Spiced Plums

Simmer all the ingredients, apart from the plums, for 10 minutes. Remove from the heat and set aside to infuse for 1 hour. Pass through a *chinois*, then bring the liquid back to the boil. Add the plums and turn down the heat to a gentle simmer, cook until they are soft. Take about a third of the plums out and blend to make the purée.

For The Parsnip Crisps

Heat the oil in a fryer to 150°C.

Using a vegetable peeler, peel the flesh of the parsnip to create lots of strips. Deep fry until lightly golden. Once cooked, dust with the blackberry powder if using.

Chef's Tip

Freeze-dried blackberry powder is available to buy online.

To Serve

Warm the rice pudding with the lemon and orange zest. Serve in bowls, adding the plum purée along with some spiced plum pieces. Garnish with the parsnip crisps.

056
THE BIRD AT BIRTLE

239 Bury & Rochdale Old Road, Birtle, OL10 4BQ

01706 540 500
www.thebirdatbirtle.co.uk Twitter: @TheBirdatBirtle Facebook: The Bird at Birtle

Lancashire fayre with flair and imagination - that's the motto of Andrew Nutter's new gastro pub The Bird at Birtle, very much the final legacy of Andrew's late father Rodney Nutter.

When Rodney handed the keys to Andrew as a Christmas present in 2015, there was clear vision to transform what was an abandoned property on the outskirts of Ashworth Valley, between Rochdale and Bury, into the iconic award-wining destination it is today.

The Bird at Birtle is little sister to Andrew's legendary Nutters Restaurant, but with a very different format and now proudly creating its own waves in the growing Manchester food scene.

"We've kept it very pubby downstairs so people can come, meet up and talk like the good old days, but then take the stairway and you're immediately hit with the fabulous atmosphere, surroundings and views across the valley," says Andrew.

Using the local surroundings Andrew and his head chef Carl Tait, an 18 year veteran of Nutters Restaurant, have created a menu that people keep coming back for, pushing the boundaries with the impact in flavour.

Another veteran from Nutters, Hannah Powell, who started washing up at Nutters at 14 years old, now leads the front of house alongside bar maestro Andy Hoyle, showcasing their managerial talents and knowledge of the menu, the local ales and the cocktails served.

The Bird at Birtle promises to deliver sumptuous, flavoursome dishes, local cask ales and heart-warming drinks in a welcoming and relaxed atmosphere.

To the Restaurant

THAI STYLE MUSSELS

SERVES 2

 *Giddy Goose Sauvignon Blanc
(England)*

Ingredients

Mussels

2 tbsp olive oil
1 small red onion (sliced)
1 red chilli (deseeded, finely chopped)
1 clove garlic (finely chopped)
fresh root ginger (knob of, finely chopped)
1 kaffir lime leaf (finely shredded)
½ stalk lemongrass (finely chopped)
1.2kg mussels
250ml dry white wine

To Finish

50g coconut cream
1 tbsp coriander (roughly chopped)
1 lime (squeeze of)

To Serve

hot crusty bread

Method

For The Mussels

Heat the olive oil in a large saucepan. Add the onion, chilli, garlic, ginger, lime leaf and lemongrass and *sauté* for 3-4 minutes until softened.

Add the mussels and white wine and cover. Cook over a high heat for approximately 4 minutes, shaking the pan frequently until the mussels open.

To Finish And Serve

Transfer the mussels to warmed serving bowls. Add the coconut cream and coriander to the cooking *liquor* in the pan. Bring to the boil, season to taste, then pour over the mussels and serve immediately with a squeeze of fresh lime. A simple but elegant dish - make sure you have some hot crusty bread ready at the end to mop up the juices.

Chef's Tip

Do try and source the kaffir lime leaf for authenticity. Any left over can be frozen and kept for future use.

SLOW BRAISED FEATHER BLADE, TRUFFLE CHIPS, BUTTERNUT SQUASH PUREE

SERVES 4

🍷 *Goldrush Pale Ale, Serious Brewing Company (England)*

Ingredients

Feather Blade

1 tbsp olive oil
1kg beef feather blade (trimmed)
1 small onion (chopped)
1 carrot (diced)
1 stick celery (chopped)
4 cloves garlic (roughly chopped)
300ml red wine
700ml beef stock (approximately)
2 tbsp tomato purée
2 sprigs fresh rosemary
few sprigs fresh thyme

Truffle Chips

2 King Edward potatoes
vegetable oil (for frying)
30g fresh Parmesan (grated)
white truffle oil (few splashes of)

Butternut Squash Purée

1 butternut squash (trimmed)
2 tbsp olive oil
cumin (pinch of)
50g butter
salt and pepper

To Serve

seasonal greens

Method

For The Feather Blade (Prepare ahead)

Preheat the oven to 160°C.

Heat the olive oil in a casserole pan and seal the feather blade on all sides. Season, add the root vegetables and garlic, and lightly colour.

Pour in the red wine and enough beef stock to cover the piece of meat. Add the tomato purée, rosemary and thyme, then cover with a *cartouche* and a lid. Place in the oven for about 3 hours until tender. Leave to cool slightly. When cool enough to handle, place the blade on a sheet of cling film and roll into a cylinder shape. Refrigerate overnight.

Strain the beef cooking *liquor* through a sieve and reduce until it slightly thickens to a coating consistency.

For The Truffle Chips

Cut the potatoes into neat batons and *blanch* in vegetable oil (120°C) for approximately 15 minutes until cooked through. Set aside.

For The Butternut Squash Purée

Preheat the oven to 180°C.

Cut the butternut in half, remove the seeds, chop into rough pieces and place in a roasting tray. Sprinkle with olive oil and cumin and roast for 15 minutes until soft. Place the squash in a blender with the butter and blend until smooth. Season to taste.

To Serve

Preheat the oven to 180°C.

Remove the cling film from the feather blade, then slice into 4. Place on an oiled tray and roast for 10 minutes until hot.

Reheat the vegetable oil to 180°C. Fry the chips in the oil for 2-3 minutes until golden, then shower with Parmesan and truffle oil. Serve alongside the beef with the purée and a portion of seasonal greens.

Chef's Tip

A great favourite all year round at The Bird, just change the accompanying vegetables to complement the season.

CHOCOLATE ORANGE TORTE

SERVES 4

Manchester Gin
& Ledger's Tangerine Tonic

Ingredients

Base

1 sheet chocolate sponge
1 tablespoon Grand Marnier

Chocolate Indulgence Filling

3 egg yolks
40g caster sugar
280g dark chocolate (40% cocoa solids)
350ml whipping cream

Ganache

200g dark chocolate (40% solids)
200ml whipping cream

To Finish

Grand Marnier ice cream
orange segments
chocolate sauce

4 x 6cm metal pastry rings

Method

For The Base

Cut the chocolate sponge into discs 6cm in diameter and use to line the metal pastry rings. Sprinkle with the Grand Marnier and allow it to soak into the sponge.

For The Chocolate Indulgence Filling

Whisk together the egg yolks and sugar until light and fluffy.

Melt the chocolate over a *bain-marie* with half the cream and stir until smooth.

Whip the remaining cream to soft peaks.

Fold the chocolate mix gently through the egg and sugar mix, then fold in the remaining cream. Pipe into the lined pastry rings and refrigerate for about 4 hours until set.

For The Ganache

Melt together the chocolate and cream over a *bain-marie* and whisk until glossy.

Unmould the tortes from the rings, then pour the ganache over the top. Leave to set in the fridge for 1 hour.

Finish with some additional chocolate sauce, orange segments and ice cream.

Chef's Tip

A decadent indulgence of chocolate and orange. What's not to like? Not a fan of orange? Substitute for some diced stem root ginger, which will give the dessert a subtle fiery kick.

066
THE BISTRO AT THE DISTILLERY

The Lakes Distillery, Setmurthy, Near Bassenthwaite Lake, Cumbria, CA13 9SJ

017687 88850 (Option 2)
www.bistroatthedistillery.com Twitter: @LakesDistillery Facebook: The Lakes Distillery

Andy Beaton began his culinary career from a very early age watching his grandad, who was originally a chef in the Polish army, taking the lead and cooking from scratch at home - in particular he remembers his grandad's infamous roast potatoes!

Initially Andy started at a local college in Barrow, before quickly gaining recognition for serious potential. At 16 years old, he ventured down to Oxford to train with none other than Raymond Blanc at Le Petit Blanc, where he learnt to treasure the most humble ingredients and develop a style that has now become his signature.

Andy enjoyed eight years at the 5 star 2 AA Rosette Miller Howe Hotel in Windermere as head chef gaining a reputation for classic, clean British cuisine. Not only did he cook for Her Majesty the Queen during his time there, but he also met his wife Paulina who ran front of house.

The first time Andy had been involved in a brand new restaurant was The Bistro at The Distillery. He described the opening "like all my Christmases had come at once" - being able to source suppliers, equipment and staff in his own vision. He continues to enjoy the creativity and flexibility given to him at The Bistro, guided by Terry Laybourne, to create the informal, relaxed and modern dining experience.

Embracing the spirit of the Lake District, regional ingredients are used where possible, with the focus on freshness, flavour and simplicity. Michelin Good Food Guide for 2016 and 2017, Open Table Diners' Choice Awards consistently.

GRILLED SCALLOPS, WILD GARLIC BUTTER

SERVES 4

🍷 *Riesling, Jean Biecher et Fils 2015 Saint Hippolyte*
(Alsace, France)

Ingredients

Wild Garlic Butter

50g wild garlic leaves
250g unsalted butter
salt and pepper

Pea Purée

500g frozen garden peas
100g unsalted butter
salt and pepper

Scallops

8 large scallops (removed from the shell, cleaned)
salt (pinch of)
rapeseed oil (drizzle of)

Garnish

4 slices crispy pancetta
1 whole lemon (cut into wedges)
pea shoots

Method

For The Wild Garlic Butter

Put the butter into a Robot Coupe or food processor and gradually add the wild garlic until it is smooth and thoroughly mixed together. Season with salt and pepper. Roll the butter into a cylinder shape in cling film and place in the fridge to firm up.

For The Pea Purée

Put the peas in a pan, cover with boiling water and leave for 1 minute. Strain the peas and transfer to a Thermomix or blender and blend on full power for 3 minutes, adding the butter gradually. Season with salt and pass through a fine sieve.

For The Scallops

Season the scallops with salt and sear on both sides in a very hot pan with a little rapeseed oil, then remove from the pan.

To Serve

Place a tablespoon of the pea purée in a cleaned scallop shell, arrange 2 scallops on top of the purée and a slice of the wild garlic butter. Place under a hot grill for 1 minute or until the butter has melted and started to bubble.

Set onto a serving plate, grate the zest of the lemon onto the scallops, along with broken up pieces of crispy pancetta. Garnish with fresh pea shoots and a wedge of fresh lemon.

Chef's Tip

Always use diver caught scallops to ensure the best produce.

BEST END OF SPRING LAMB, COURGETTE & BASIL PUREE

SERVES 4

🍷 *Gassies 2010 Château Rauzan-Gassies, Margaux
(Bordeaux, France)*

Ingredients

4 x 3 bone racks of spring lamb (*French trimmed*)

Semi-Dried Plum Tomatoes

6 plum tomatoes (halved)
salt (pinch of)
sugar (pinch of)
1 clove garlic (finely sliced)
6 sprigs thyme
olive oil

Courgette And Basil Purée

4 courgettes (cut into 1cm dice)
100ml olive oil
50g fresh basil leaves
salt (to season)

Noisette Potatoes

2 large potatoes
butter (large knob of)
2 sprigs thyme
1 clove garlic
salt (to season)

Courgettes

2 courgettes
olive oil (drizzle of)
salt (to season)

To Serve

black olives
fine green beans

Method

For The Semi-Dried Plum Tomatoes (Prepare ahead)

Season the tomatoes with salt and sugar, then place a slice of garlic on each of the halves. Place a sprig of thyme on each tomato, drizzle with olive oil and put in a warm place for 24 hours until they become semi-dried. Alternatively, dry in a low oven (60°C) overnight.

For The Courgette And Basil Purée

Heat the oil in a pan, add the courgettes and cook on a medium heat for about 20 minutes, stirring from time to time.

Blanch the basil leaves in boiling water, then plunge straight into ice water.

When the courgettes are soft, transfer them with the basil to a Thermomix or blender. Blitz on full power for 3 minutes until really smooth. Season, then pass through a fine sieve.

For The Noisette Potatoes

Using a melon baller, cut out ball shaped pieces from the potatoes. Pan roast in foaming butter with the thyme and garlic. Season with salt.

For The Courgettes

Using a melon baller, cut ball shapes from the courgettes. Cook quickly in oil and season with salt.

For The Lamb

Preheat the oven to 180°C (fan).

Render the fat from the lamb racks in a hot pan until it is nice and crispy. Transfer the lamb to the oven and roast for 7-8 minutes, or longer if you prefer well done.

> **Chef's Tip**
> Cover the lamb bones with tin foil when cooking to ensure they don't burn in the cooking process.

To Serve

Assemble and serve as pictured.

WHISKY PANNA COTTA, RASPBERRIES, HONEYCOMB

SERVES 6

🍷 *The ONE Whisky*
(Cumbria, England)

Ingredients

Whisky Panna Cotta Cream

300ml uht whipping cream
112ml uht whole milk
1 vanilla pod (scraped)
1 strip lemon zest
112g sugar
3 leaves bronze gelatine (soaked in cold water)
150ml The ONE whisky

Raspberry Gel

250g raspberry purée
3g agar agar
50g caster sugar
½ lemon (juice of)

Honeycomb

80g sugar
12g honey
33g glucose
15ml water
4g bicarbonate of soda

Garnish

fresh raspberries
mint leaves
viola flowers

6 timbale moulds

Method

For The Whisky Panna Cotta Cream (Prepare ahead)

Boil together the cream, milk, vanilla and lemon zest, then reduce to a simmer for 1 minute. Remove from the heat and add the sugar, gelatine and whisky. Set over ice so the vanilla does not sink to the bottom of the moulds. Pour into the moulds and chill for a few hours until set.

Chef's Tip

Always use The ONE whisky to ensure the best taste.

For The Raspberry Gel

Mix together the raspberry purée, agar agar and sugar in a pan. Bring to the boil, then remove from the heat and chill. When cold, blitz in a Thermomix or food processor with the lemon juice to a gel consistency. Pass through a fine sieve.

For The Honeycomb

Boil together the sugar, honey, glucose and water in a pan and heat to 120°C to make a caramel.

Whisk the bicarbonate of soda into the mix, half at a time. Empty the contents of the pan into a tray lined with baking paper. Leave to set.

To Serve

Serve as pictured.

076
THE BLACK SWAN HOTEL

Ravenstonedale, Kirkby Stephen, Cumbria, CA17 4NG

015396 23204
www.blackswanhotel.com Twitter: @BlackSwanEden Facebook: The Black Swan Ravenstonedale
Head chef: Twitter: @scottsfoodworld Facebook: Scott Fairweather

The Black Swan is situated in the beautiful conservation village of Ravenstonedale, nestled in the Howgill Fells at the heart of the Eden valley between the Yorkshire Dales and the Lake District, Cumbria. It is ideally situated for exploring the area and easily accessible from the M6; just a five minute drive.

Since being acquired by the Dinnes family in 2006, this popular pub with rooms has gone from strength to strength, winning many national awards including AA Pub of the Year for England, Good Hotel Guide Cesar Award and Sawdays 'Special Places to Stay'. Along with their loyal and dedicated staff, Louise and team have worked tirelessly to create a 'traditional meets quirky' pub, aimed at the weary traveller, local punter and food connoisseur alike, ensuring a home-from-home, informal environment with exceptional, friendly service.

The Black Swan has 16 individually decorated bedrooms, five of which are dog friendly and also have disabled access, as well as a further three garden glamping tents in the summer season for the more adventurous amongst us. The building is split into many intimate rooms;

a well-stocked bar, cosy lounge with a log burning fire, two small dining rooms and a spacious garden for which to enjoy the late summer nights.

The food offering is designed by local Cumbrian head chef Scott Fairweather, whose aim is to provide 'something for everyone' whilst sticking firmly to the pub surroundings. The kitchen is driven by seasonality and provides freshly prepared, locally sourced ingredients on a menu which is creatively put together.

The Black Swan comes as a pleasant surprise to guests who may stumble across it or indeed those who make a special trip. The hotel's goal is to undersell and over deliver, providing an environment where you can embrace and enjoy the wholesome package that the pub prides itself on.

Louise and co have worked tirelessly to create a 'traditional meets quirky' pub, aimed at the weary traveller, local punter and food connoisseur alike, ensuring a home-from-home, informal environment with exceptional, friendly service.

GOAT'S CHEESE, GINGERBREAD, BEETROOT, RASPBERRY

SERVES 4-6

 Domaine Daulny Sancerre, Loire, 2014
(France)

Ingredients

Gingerbread

200g self-raising flour
table salt (pinch of)
4 tsp ground ginger
1 tsp ground nutmeg
1 tsp mixed spice
200g golden syrup
100g black treacle
150g porridge oats
150g unsalted butter
150g light brown sugar
2 eggs
1 tbsp semi-skimmed milk

Balsamic Vinegar Jelly

150ml balsamic vinegar
50g caster sugar
3g agar agar

Golden Beetroot Purée

1kg golden beetroot (similar in size)
2 sprigs thyme
1 tbsp sea salt
6 whole black peppercorns

Pickled Beetroot

2 large beetroot
500ml red wine vinegar
125g caster sugar

Garnish

400g soft goat's cheese of your choice (torn into
bite-size pieces)
fresh raspberries
2 large candy beetroot (sliced thinly, cut into
4cm discs)
nasturtium leaves

30cm square baking tray (lined with
greaseproof paper)

Method

For The Gingerbread

Preheat the oven to 170°C (fan).

Sieve the flour, salt, ginger, nutmeg and mixed spice into a mixing bowl. Place the golden syrup, treacle, porridge oats and butter into a saucepan and heat gently until melted. Remove from the stove, stir in the sugar then whisk in the eggs and milk until fully incorporated. Fold in the dry ingredients, then pour into the prepared baking tray. Bake for 25-35 minutes until firm, using a cocktail stick to test the centre. Cool on a wire rack before dicing.

For The Balsamic Vinegar Jelly

Whisk all of the ingredients together in a large saucepan and bring up to the boil. Pass through a fine sieve onto a baking tray or shallow dish lined with greaseproof paper and leave to set until firm. Peel away from the paper and slice into ½cm squares ready to serve.

For The Golden Beetroot Purée

Place the whole beetroots into a large pan with the thyme, salt and peppercorns, then cover with cold water. Boil for 1 hour or until completely soft, then drain and peel once cool enough to handle. Slice into wedges and blend in a food processor for 3 minutes, adding hot water to achieve a smooth purée. Pass through a fine sieve, season with salt to taste.

For The Pickled Beetroot

Slice the beetroot as thinly as possible, either by hand or on a mandoline, then cut into 4cm discs. Bring the vinegar and sugar to the boil in a saucepan and simmer for 5 minutes to dissolve. Add the discs, cook until *al dente*, then drain through a sieve, reserving the pickling *liquor*. Allow both the beetroot and pickle to cool separately, then combine. The beetroot will keep for up to 1 week.

To Serve

Place 5 teaspoons of golden beetroot purée onto a plate, followed by the torn goat's cheese, diced gingerbread and balsamic jelly squares. Finish with fresh raspberries, then the discs of pickled and raw beetroot and the nasturtium leaves.

Chef's Tip

Serve all the elements at room temperature to benefit from the maximum flavour.

CRAB RISOTTO, RADISH, CREME FRAICHE, PONZU & LIME DRESSING

SERVES 4

 La Lejania Chardonnay, 2014
(Chile)

Ingredients

Crab Stock

4 tbsp olive oil
1 onion (peeled, sliced)
2 cloves garlic (crushed)
1 stick celery (peeled, sliced)
1 carrot (peeled, sliced)
1 bulb fennel (sliced)
shells from 2 crabs
1 tbsp tomato purée
2 bay leaves
1 tsp white peppercorns
1 lemon (juice of)

Risotto Base

8 shallots (peeled, finely diced)
4 cloves garlic (peeled, grated)
2 tbsp olive oil
800g arborio rice
1 glass white wine
crab stock (hot)
4 tbsp crème fraîche
100g Parmesan (finely grated)

Dressed Crab

200g white crab meat
4 tbsp crème fraîche

Ponzu And Lime Dressing

200ml Japanese ponzu
50ml elderflower cordial
50ml lime juice
Ultratex (to thicken)

Garnish

8 radishes (thinly sliced)
chives (snipped)
extra virgin olive oil

Method

For The Crab Stock

Heat the oil and sweat the vegetables in a large saucepan until softened. Add the crab shells and smash with the end of a rolling pin to break them down as much as possible. Stir in the tomato purée, followed by the bay leaves, peppercorns and lemon juice, then cover with 4 litres of water and leave to simmer gently for 2 hours. Skim any fat from the surface with a ladle, then pass the stock through a fine sieve ready to cook the risotto base.

For The Risotto Base

Gently sweat the shallots and garlic in a wide *sauté* pan over a low heat in the oil until softened. Add the rice to the pan and stir well to lightly toast the grains. Add the white wine and stir until almost completely reduced, then ladle in the hot crab stock, small amounts at a time, stirring continuously while the risotto cooks. Continue to add stock, reduce and stir until the rice is cooked *al dente*. Finish by stirring in the crème fraîche and grated Parmesan. Leave to stand for 2-3 minutes off the heat before serving.

For The Dressed Crab

Place the crab meat onto a tray and carefully pick through for small pieces of shell. Place the picked meat into a cloth and squeeze out as much excess moisture as possible. Turn out into a mixing bowl and stir in crème fraîche to bind the meat together. Serve at room temperature.

For The Ponzu And Lime Dressing

Place all the liquid ingredients into a mixing bowl and whisk together. Whisk in the Ultratex, 1 tablespoon at a time, until thickened to a vinaigrette consistency.

To Serve

Spoon the risotto into bowls and dress with the ponzu dressing. This is used as a seasoning for the whole dish. Place small piles of the dressed crab meat on top, followed by radish slices, snipped chives and a good drizzle of extra virgin olive oil.

Chef's Tip

This risotto can also be used as a garnish to other fantastic pieces of fish that are available; try it alongside some roasted halibut or cod loin for a show-stopping dinner party dish.

LEMON MERINGUE, PASSION FRUIT, TOASTED COCONUT

SERVES 4

 Petit Guiraud Sauternes, 2012
(France)

Ingredients

Passion Fruit Purée

250g Boiron passion fruit purée
50g caster sugar
4g agar agar

Lemon Mousse

2 lemon (zest and juice of)
60g egg yolks
100g caster sugar
4 gelatine leaves (soaked in cold water)
400ml double cream

French Meringue

120g egg whites
200g caster sugar

Italian Meringue

120g caster sugar
2 tbsp water
1 tbsp liquid glucose
60g egg whites

Garnish

toasted, desiccated coconut
freeze-dried passion fruit pieces
lemons (for zesting)
micro lemon balm cress

15cm x 23cm baking tray or plastic container
(lined with greaseproof paper)

Chef's Tip

This lemon mousse recipe freezes very well if you want to get ahead on preparation or to save any extra for another day.

Method

For The Passion Fruit Purée

Whisk all the ingredients together in a saucepan and bring to the boil. Pour out onto a baking tray and leave to cool completely. Once set, transfer to a food processor and blend for 3 minutes until smooth. Pass through a fine sieve and store in a squeezy bottle.

For The Lemon Mousse

Place the lemon zest and juice into a small saucepan and boil to reduce by half. Pass through a sieve and set aside. Whisk the egg yolks and sugar in a bowl over a *bain-marie* until thickened and doubled in volume, known as a *sabayon*. Remove from the heat, squeeze the excess water from the gelatine and whisk into the warm *sabayon* to dissolve. Stir in the lemon juice, then leave to cool to room temperature. Whisk the cream to soft peaks and gently fold into the cooled mix, being careful not to beat the air out of the mix. Transfer to a 15cm x 23cm baking tray or plastic container lined with greaseproof paper. Level off the top of the mix and leave to set in the fridge for 4 hours before slicing.

For The French Meringue (Prepare ahead)

Preheat the oven to 50°C (fan).

Whisk the egg whites and sugar together on full speed in an electric mixer until thick and glossy. Line a large baking tray with greaseproof paper and, using a palette knife, spread a thin layer of meringue evenly across it. Dry out in an oven overnight to leave a crisp, clean, white meringue. Break into shards before serving.

For The Italian Meringue

Place the sugar, water and glucose into a saucepan and boil to 121°C, using a digital probe. Meanwhile, whisk the egg whites in an electric mixer on full speed until they are doubled in size and pale white in colour. Slowly trickle in the sugar syrup and continue to whisk until the meringue has cooled to room temperature, about 15-20 minutes. Spoon the thick, glossy meringue into a piping bag and store in the fridge until needed. This must be made fresh on the day of serving for best results.

To Serve

Squeeze the passion fruit purée into a serving bowl, then pipe on the Italian meringue and lightly blow torch until golden; it will toast as easily as a marshmallow. Cut the lemon mousse into 12cm x 3cm rectangles and roll 4 of them in toasted coconut shavings. Arrange on the plate and garnish as pictured.

086
THE CON CLUB

48 Greenwood Street, Altrincham, Cheshire, WA14 1RZ

0161 696 6870
www.conclubuk.com Twitter: @ConClubAlty

This grand old building has stood at the heart of Altrincham since 1887 and for the first 120 years or so of its life it was home to Altrincham Working Men's Conservative Club. The club closed some years ago and the building lay unloved before being restored and revived in 2016 by chef-restaurateur and local resident David Vanderhook.

These days The Con Club welcomes those of all political persuasions and since opening in November 2016 has made a name for simple, high quality dining in a buzzing, food-hall setting. Renowned for fantastic sushi, alongside fabulous local meat cooked on the charcoal grill, head chef Dax Gee and his team have developed close relationships with local suppliers, including the traders at Altrincham Market across the street, and they take pride in creating daily specials in response to seasonal availability.

The Con Club is also a thriving bar open late into the night. There is a wide range of fine wines, spirits, cocktails and beers on offer and an on-site microbrewery named 'Federation', in honour of the former brewery in Gateshead which was established to supply beer to working men's clubs in the North of England.

Although still a new business, The Con Club is well on its way to becoming a fixture in Altrincham and the management and staff are proud to be part of the regeneration of this historic town.

SEARED TUNA TATAKI, MISO TRUFFLE PONZU DRESSING, MINT, CORIANDER & SPRING ONION SALAD WITH PINEAPPLE DRESSING

SERVES 4

 Ginjo Sake (Japan)
Serve chilled.

Ingredients

Tuna Tataki

600g ahi grade tuna
blackened Cajun pepper

Miso Truffle Ponzu Dressing

50g white miso paste
50ml ponzu vinegar (cider will do)
50ml dark soy sauce
50ml yuzu juice
50ml truffle oil

Pineapple Dressing

300g dark brown sugar
500ml water
100ml ponzu vinegar
3 lemongrass stalks (crushed)
100ml fresh pineapple juice
100ml vegetable oil

Spring Onion Salad

½ pomegranate (seeds of)
1 spring onion (finely sliced diagonally)
coriander and mint (picked)
Maldon sea salt (pinch of)

Garnish

viola flowers

Method

For The Tuna Tataki

Trim the tuna into one long rectangular block approximately 20cm x 3cm. Cover with blackened Cajun pepper and sear in a very hot pan for 15 seconds each side. Refrigerate immediately.

Chef's Tip

Refrigerate the tuna immediately after searing in the pan.

For The Miso Truffle Ponzu Dressing

Mix the miso paste and vinegar together in a bowl. Add the soy sauce and continue mixing, then add the yuzu juice and continue whisking. Lastly, pour in the truffle oil and mix until combined.

For The Pineapple Dressing

Add all the ingredients, except the oil, into a pan and simmer on a low heat for 30-40 minutes to your desired consistency. Strain the mixture into a jug, then slowly mix in the oil with a hand blender. Leave to cool.

To Serve

Slice the tuna into blocks 1cm thick. Mix all the salad ingredients together and add the pineapple dressing to taste. Plate as shown and, just before serving, shake the ponzu dressing and pour sparingly over the tuna. Garnish with edible viola flowers.

SUMMER BEEF: CONFIT BRISKET, CRISPY OX CHEEK, DANDELION & BURDOCK GLAZED LONG RIB, BARRELED OXTAIL, SUMMER BEANS, SAUTEED KIDNEY

SERVES 4

 Château Musar
(Lebanon)

Ingredients

Barreled Oxtail

1 oxtail (sliced)
2 sticks celery, 2 carrots (finely diced)
chives, flat leaf parsley (handful of, finely chopped)
butter (knob of)

Confit Brisket

1½kg brisket (boned, rolled), 2kg dripping/*confit* oil
2 carrots, 2 onions, 1 leek (roughly chopped)
2 sprigs rosemary and thyme, ½ bulb garlic

Glazed Rib And Crispy Ox Cheek

1 long-cut short-rib from the flank, ½ ox cheek
2 carrots (sliced lengthways)
1 onion, 2 sticks celery, 1 leek (roughly chopped)
1 whole bulb garlic (roasted)
1 bay leaf, 15g thyme, 250ml red wine
1 litre beef stock
1 litre dandelion and burdock
250g mashed potato, chives (handful of, snipped)
parsley (few sprigs, chopped)
3 spring onions (sliced), salt and pepper
egg (beaten), 100g panko, 100g polenta (combined)
(to *pane*)
oil (to deep fry)

Summer Beans And Kidney

butter (knob of), 100g ox kidney (diced)
100g broad beans (peeled), 100g fresh peas (shelled)
2 banana shallots (finely diced), salt and pepper
lemon juice (spritz of), chives (finely chopped)

Jus

400ml red wine, 50g redcurrant jelly
beef stock (reserved from ox cheek)

Method

For The Barreled Oxtail (Prepare ahead)

Preheat the oven to 140ºC (fan).
Roast the oxtail and vegetables for 3 hours. Pick the meat from the bones, add the vegetables and herbs, roll in cling film into a sausage shape and set overnight. When ready to serve, slice into 9cm pieces, remove the cling film and reheat in foaming butter.

For The Confit Brisket (Prepare ahead)

Preheat the oven to 120ºC (fan).
Seal the brisket all over in a deep tray, add the other ingredients, and roast for 4 hours. Remove from the oil and drain. Wrap tightly in cling film and refrigerate for 6 hours. To serve, slice and reheat in the oven.

For The Glazed Rib And Crispy Ox Cheek (Prepare ahead)

Seal the meat all over in a deep, oiled pan. Add the vegetables, bay and thyme, cook for 2 minutes. *Deglaze* with the wine, add the stock and gently braise for 2½ hours.
Remove the rib, cheek and carrot and set aside. Strain the liquid and discard the vegetables.
Reduce 500ml of the beef stock with the dandelion and burdock to a syrupy glaze.
When cool enough to handle, remove the rib bone, brush with the glaze and refrigerate. Once set, cut into equal pieces. Reheat in a pan and brush with more glaze.
Pick the cheek meat into the mashed potato, along with the carrot (diced), chives, parsley, spring onions and seasoning. Mix well. Line a baking tray with cling film, press the mix into it and refrigerate for 2 hours. Cut into equal pieces, *pane* with the egg mix, then the panko and polenta mix. Deep fry for 2 minutes, then cook in the oven for 2 minutes (180ºC fan). Slice diagonally.

For The Summer Beans And Kidney

Add the butter to a hot pan. When foaming, seal the kidney for 5 seconds, then add the beans, peas and shallots, cook on a medium heat for 2 minutes. Season, then add the lemon and chives.

For The Jus

Add the wine and jelly to a hot pan, burn off the alcohol, then add the stock. Bring to the boil, then simmer and reduce to a gravy consistency, skim the fat. Pass through a muslin cloth.

To Serve

Serve as pictured.

DAIRY-FREE CARROT CAKE, PASSION FRUIT GEL, PASSION FRUIT CRISP, CRYSTALLISED PECANS

SERVES 8

 Brockmans Gin Negroni

Ingredients

Carrot Cake

Bowl 1:
160g plain flour (sieved)
1-2 tbsp cinnamon powder
10g bicarbonate of soda
50g pecans (chopped)
50g dessicated coconut

Bowl 2:
200ml vegetable oil
1 large whole egg
240g caster sugar
20g egg yolk

Bowl 3:
300g carrot (finely grated)

Bowl 4:
60g egg white

Passion Fruit Gel And Crisps

260g passion fruit purée
100ml stock syrup
20g Ultratex or Sosa Gel

Crystallised Pecans

175g pecan nuts
40ml dark rum
100g icing sugar

To Serve

high quality coconut sorbet (we use a fabulous
local supplier - Dunham Massey Farm ice cream)
edible flowers/micro coriander
toasted Italian meringue (optional)

20cm square baking tin (lined with parchment)

Method

For The Carrot Cake

Preheat the oven to 160°C (fan).

Mix the ingredients of bowl 1. Whisk and *emulsify* the
ingredients of bowl 2. Combine bowl 1 into bowl 2 and mix well.
Add the carrot from bowl 3 and combine. Whisk the egg whites
of bowl 4 until the soft peak stage and fold into the rest of the
mixture. Pour into the cake tin and bake for around 30 minutes
until a knife comes out clean. Cool on a baking rack.

> **Chef's Tip**
>
> Get all your cake ingredients into separate bowls as detailed
> to make life easy!

For The Passion Fruit Gel And Crisps (Prepare ahead)

Blend all the ingredients to a gel consistency. Transfer to a
squeezy bottle.

Spread some of the gel thinly onto a silicone mat and dehydrate
until crisp in the bottom of a low oven (60°C fan).

For The Crystallised Pecans

Preheat the oven to 170°C (fan).

Roast the nuts for around 2 minutes until toasted.

Bring the rum and icing sugar to the boil in a stainless steel pan,
then reduce for 30 seconds. Add the pecans and stir continuously
with a large metal spoon until dry and crystallised. Pour onto a
lined baking tray and spread out evenly. Leave to cool.

To Serve

Place a slice of carrot cake onto the plate, then pipe passion
fruit gel dots around. Add a few pecans and set a *quenelle* of
sorbet on top of the cake. Garnish with the passion fruit crisps
and micro coriander and/or edible viola flowers.

Optional: Serve with soft Italian meringue lightly toasted with a
blow torch - it adds a great texture to the dish.

096
EL GATO NEGRO TAPAS

52 King Street, Manchester, M2 4LY

0161 694 8585
www.elgatonegrotapas.com Twitter: @ElGatoNegroFood Facebook: El Gato Negro Tapas

Since last gracing the pages of Relish, chef patron Simon Shaw has taken El Gato Negro Tapas westwards across the Pennines, swapping the honeyed Yorkshire stone of Ripponden for the elegant brickwork of city centre Manchester. Aiming to retain its charm and personality and build on the success in West Yorkshire, they threw open the doors of the historic three storey townhouse on King Street after a year of extensive refurbishment.

The new home has enabled the team to fulfil the ambition of catering for a wider audience, offering both bar and casual restaurant dining across three floors; mirroring the varied, exciting experience of many of Simon's favourite establishments in Barcelona, Seville and San Sebastián.

Dedicated to finding the best produce both from Spain and locally, it uses these to create an exciting take on contemporary Spanish cuisine, serving both seasonal specials and signature tapas dishes. The menu combines modern and traditional Spanish flavours and techniques while taking inspiration from local and global sources alike. El Gato Negro's food is perfectly complemented by a superbly-curated selection of Spanish wines, sherries, spirits, tonics, beers and cocktails.

The restaurant has received popular and critical acclaim since reopening; Newcomer of the Year at the 2016 Manchester Food and Drink Festival Awards; City Restaurant of the Year at the Lancashire Life Food and Drink Awards; debuting in the National Restaurant Awards UK Top 100, and it is the only city restaurant to receive a Michelin Guide Bib Gourmand in 2017, recognising exceptionally good food at moderate prices.

Location photographs by Joby Catto

Award-winning modern tapas dishes and signature seasonal specials showcase the best of local and Spanish ingredients at El Gato Negro Tapas.

GILLARDEAU OYSTERS, YUZU JUICE, PICKLED CUCUMBER, WASABI TOBIKO

SERVES 4

🍷 Albariño de Fefiñanes 2015, Rias Baixas
(Spain)

Ingredients

4 Gillardeau oysters

Pickled Cucumber

60g cucumber
100ml rice wine vinegar

Yuzu Dressing

100ml yuzu juice
50ml ponzu juice

To Serve

60g wasabi tobiko (also known as flying fish roe)
crushed ice
seaweed (optional)

Method

For The Pickled Cucumber (Prepare 4 hours ahead)

Peel the cucumber, cut into 4 lengthways and remove the seeds. Cut into strips and finely dice (*brunoise*). Cover with the rice wine vinegar and chill.

For The Yuzu Dressing

Mix together the yuzu and ponzu and set aside.

To Prepare The Oysters And Serve

Shuck the oysters and cut through the muscle to release the oyster - be careful to remove any excess shell. Divide the yuzu and ponzu juice equally between the 4 oysters. Add the pickled cucumber and top with the wasabi tobiko. Serve on crushed ice and garnish with seaweed.

HOT & SUGAR CURED MACKEREL, CELERIAC, PINK GRAPEFRUIT

SERVES 4

Equipo Navazos 'I Think' Manzanilla En Rama 2016 (Spain)

Ingredients

Sugar Cured Mackerel

¼ pink grapefruit (zest of)
100g light brown, soft sugar
30g Maldon salt
20ml pomegranate molasses
8 mackerel fillets (4 for sugar curing, 4 for pan frying)

Baked Celeriac

1 celeriac (washed)
1 clove garlic
1 sprig thyme
salt and pepper
100ml water
lemon oil (drizzle of)
1 tbsp fresh parsley (chopped)

Pomegranate Sauce

100ml pomegranate molasses
100ml pink grapefruit juice

Garnish

1 pink grapefruit (segmented, reserve the juice for the sauce)

Method

For The Sugar Cured Mackerel (Prepare in advance)

Mix the grapefruit zest, sugar, salt and pomegranate molasses together. Place 4 of the mackerel fillets in a non-reactive tray, skin-side down, and sprinkle over the cure. Cover with cling film and place in the fridge for 12 hours. Turn the mackerel and leave for another 6-8 hours. Wash off the cure and skin the fish. Cut the fillets in half.

For The Baked Celeriac

Preheat the oven to 150°C (fan).

Place the celeriac in tin foil with the garlic, thyme, salt, pepper and water and wrap tightly. Place on a baking tray and bake for 3-4 hours until the celeriac is tender. Cut the cooked celeriac into wedges.

For The Pomegranate Sauce

Place the pomegranate molasses and grapefruit juice in a saucepan and reduce to a syrup.

To Finish And Serve

Chargrill the celeriac wedges, then roll in the lemon oil and chopped parsley. Pan fry the remaining 4 mackerel fillets and assemble the dish as pictured.

TURRON MOUSSE, PEAR, BASIL, ALMOND BRITTLE

SERVES 6-8

🍷 *Bodegas Itsasmendi Txacoli Urezti 2014 Bizkaiko Txakolina (Spain)*

Ingredients

Turron Mousse

100g cream cheese
150g mascarpone
75g fig syrup
200g turron
150ml double cream
1½ leaves gelatine (softened in ice cold water)

Basil Poaching Liquor

1 litre white wine
500ml water
150g sugar
1 lemon (juice of)
5g ascorbic acid
½ stick cinnamon
¼ pack basil
5 pears (peeled)

Pear And Basil Semi Gel

50g sugar
5g agar agar
500ml pear and basil poaching *liquor*

Almond Brittle

250g almonds
250g sugar

Pear Sorbet

200g nappage
500g pear purée

Method

For The Turron Mousse (Prepare ahead)

Beat together the cream cheese, mascarpone and fig syrup. When smooth, crumble through the turron and beat again until combined. Heat the double cream and melt in the softened gelatine. Strain the cream over the cream cheese mix and stir until combined. Pour into a large gastro or terrine and allow to set for a minimum of 4 hours. Transfer to a piping bag.

For The Basil Poaching Liquor (Prepare the day before)

In a pan, bring all the ingredients, except for the basil and pears, to the boil. Add the basil, then pour over the pears to poach. Cover with cling film and allow to sit out of the fridge overnight.

For The Pear And Basil Semi Gel (Prepare ahead)

Mix the sugar and agar agar together. Bring the pear and basil poaching *liquor* to the boil, then whisk in the sugar and agar mix. Boil for 3 minutes, then strain into a bowl and set in the fridge for a minimum of 6 hours. Once set, place into a blender and blitz to a smooth gel. Transfer to a piping bag.

For The Almond Brittle Mix

Preheat the oven to 200°C (fan).

Roast the almonds for 5 minutes and allow to cool. Whilst cooling, place the sugar into a large pan and make a direct caramel. Pour onto a non-stick mat and allow to set. Blitz the cooled almonds into nibs, then blitz the cold caramel to a fine powder. Mix the blitzed almonds and caramel together, sprinkle onto a non-stick mat and place in the oven for 4 minutes. Remove from the oven and allow to sit for 2 minutes. Shape as desired.

For The Pear Sorbet

Blitz the nappage and pear purée until well combined. Pass through a sieve and freeze in a paco container. Alternatively, churn in an ice cream machine and freeze until required.

To Serve

Serve as pictured.

106
EVUNA

277-279 Deansgate, Manchester, M3 4EW
79 Thomas Street, Northern Quarter, Manchester, M4 1LQ
46 King Street, Knutsford, WA16 6EU

Deansgate: 0161 819 2752, Northern Quarter: 0161 833 1130
www.evuna.com Twitter: @Evunamanchester Facebook: Evuna NQ & Evuna Deansgate

Evuna Restaurants have one vision - to bring the people of Manchester the many hidden gems of the amazing, diverse country that is Spain. Originating as a wine importer, in 2003 they brought the best chefs from Madrid to rustle up an eclectic mix of Spanish dishes, ranging from tapas to full banquets, with anything in between.

In Northern Quarter (NQ) and Deansgate, Evuna offer a wine merchant service where customers can take their favourite wines home with them by the bottle or by the case. In the small shop area, you can browse the offers whilst enjoying a glass of wine and some tapas.

Following the success of their current venues, Evuna are excited to announce their third location, opening in summer 2017. 46 King Street is a typical Tudor, four storey, Grade II listed building on the main lower street of historic Knutsford. The basement will house a traditional wine cellar, visible from the street outside through the glass paving. The welcoming ground floor is a bustly tapas bar in keeping with Evuna NQ, whereas the first floor offers more formal dining, with private booth seating and a 20 cover space available for private hire. To the rear of the property, there is a beautiful Spanish garden with a retractable roof, allowing the garden to be used for all year dining.

The Knutsford menu will be full tapas, main courses and paellas along with monthly specials served around the wine region themes.

Even with the growth of Evuna, it remains very much 'family' through and through. Mother Frances, along with husband and wife team Jane and Bosun, have over a decade of restaurant experience with a true passion for all things Spanish.

WINE OF THE W

SANTALBA
2012
FROM RIOJA
100% ORGANIC TEMP

BOTTLE £42
GLASS 175ml .... £11·
TAKE AWAY £32

S BAR & RESTAURANT

The food offering is wine led by their award-winning boutique wineries, resulting in monthly specials to complement the wine region of the month, whilst not forgetting delicious Spanish staples.

SUQUET DE PESCADO
CATALAN FISH STEW

SERVES 4

 Albariño
(Spain)

Ingredients

Picada

10 raw almonds
2 slices freshly baked bread
4 cloves garlic
saffron (pinch of)

Sauce

olive oil (drizzle of)
1 tbsp garlic (minced)
2 tomatoes (minced)
250g potatoes (peeled, cut into small pieces)
120ml white wine
700ml homemade fish stock (or good quality shop bought)
½ tbsp paprika
salt and pepper

Seafood

100g hake (or white fish)
200g squid
300g prawns
300g fresh mussels or clams

Garnish

lemon wedges
chopped parsley

Method

For The Picada

Toast the almonds, bread, garlic and saffron in a pan. Blend in a food processor to a thick paste.

For The Sauce

Heat the oil in a saucepan, then add the garlic and tomatoes. *Sauté* for 5 minutes, then add the potatoes, wine and fish stock, ensuring that the potatoes are covered with liquid. Add salt and the paprika and cook for 20 minutes on a medium heat until the potatoes are soft. Season to taste.

To Finish The Dish

Add the fish and squid to the stew and cook for 3 minutes uncovered. Add the prawns and mussels or clams and cook until the shellfish open and the prawns are pink. Do not overcook the seafood. Garnish with lemon wedges and chopped parsley.

Chef's Tip

Be careful not to overcook the seafood and serve immediately.

ORANGE & FENNEL MARINATED PORK BELLY, CARROT PUREE, CARAMELISED ORANGE

SERVES 4

🍷 *Viña Solorca Crianza, Ribera del Duero (Spain)*

Ingredients

Pork Belly

1kg boned pork belly
2 whole large, sweet oranges
50g fennel seeds
1 litre premium orange juice

Carrot Purée

5 carrots (peeled)
olive oil (drizzle of)
500ml whole milk
125g salted butter
salt and pepper

Pork And Orange Jus

pork belly cooking liquids
250ml red wine

Caramelised Orange

1 large, sweet orange (peeled)
sugar (to dust)

To Serve

sautéed potatoes
rocket

kitchen blow torch

Method

For The Pork Belly (Allow 3 days)

Place the pork belly in a baking tray. Cut the oranges into thick slices and place on the pork belly. Spread the fennel seeds on the top and season with salt and pepper. Place in the fridge for 24 hours.

Preheat the oven to 160°C.

Add the orange juice to the roasting tray with the pork belly and pour in enough water to cover the pork. Cover with tin foil and roast for 3-4 hours until the meat is tender.

When the meat is soft, remove the liquid from the tray and set aside. Press the pork belly with another roasting tray. Place in the fridge for 24 hours.

Preheat the oven to 180°C.

Portion the belly to the required size. Pan fry until golden brown on both sides, then place in the oven for 10 minutes.

> **Chef's Tip**
>
> This dish takes 3 days to prepare so plan well ahead. Marinate the pork belly on day 1. Roast the pork belly, press it and cool it on day 2. On day 3, portion and serve.

For The Carrot Purée

Slice the carrots thinly. Place in a hot pan with a drizzle of olive oil and *sauté* until golden. Add the milk and butter and cook until the carrots are soft. Transfer the carrots to a food processor and blitz with enough liquid until you get the required consistency. Season to taste.

For The Pork And Orange Jus

Combine the cooking liquids from the pork belly. Add the red wine and bring to the boil. Simmer until reduced to your desired consistency.

For The Caramelised Orange

Slice the orange into small wedges. Toss in sugar and burn with a blow torch until the sugar caramelises.

To Serve

Serve as pictured.

TORRIJA CARAMELIZADA
TRADITIONAL CARAMELISED BREAD FRITTER, CHOCOLATE SAUCE

SERVES 4

Muscatel
(Spain)

Ingredients

Caramelised Bread Fritter

1 litre whole milk
3 tbsp sugar
1 stick cinnamon
1 lemon (zest of)
4 pieces bread (1 day old)
3-4 eggs (beaten)
300g plain flour
oil (drizzle of)
brown sugar (to sprinkle)
ground cinnamon (to sprinkle)

Chocolate Sauce

500ml whole milk
300g chocolate (75% cocoa solids, chopped)

To Serve

vanilla ice cream

Garnish

strawberries
orange segments

Method

For The Caramelised Bread Fritter (Torrija)

Put the milk, sugar, cinnamon stick and lemon zest in a pan, bring to the boil and leave to infuse for 5 minutes. Place the slices of bread in a baking dish. Discard the cinnamon stick and pour the milk over the bread. Leave to soak for a few minutes.

Preheat the oven to 180°C.

Dip the bread in the beaten egg, then pass through the flour. Lightly fry in a little oil for 3-4 minutes on each side until brown. Lay the bread in an ovenproof dish, sprinkle generously with sugar and ground cinnamon and place in the oven for 5 minutes.

For The Chocolate Sauce

Bring the milk to the boil, add the chocolate to melt it, then remove from the heat and stir well.

To Serve

Drizzle the sauce over the hot fritters and serve with vanilla ice cream. Garnish with strawberries and orange segments.

Chef's Tip
Experiment with different milks for a dairy free alternative.

GEORGE & DRAGON

Clifton, Penrith, Cumbria, CA10 2ER

01768 865 381
www.georgeanddragonclifton.co.uk Twitter: @GeorgeDragonCli Facebook: George And Dragon Clifton

The George and Dragon was transformed in 2008 when it was taken on by Charles Lowther. It has since built up an excellent reputation for its sustainable food philosophy, growing and rearing much of its own produce on the Lowther family estate.

The gardens at their nearby sister establishment, Askham Hall (gardens, café, restaurant and hotel www.askhamhall.co.uk), are home to a wide variety of fruit, vegetables, edible flowers, rare-breed pigs and goats, pedigree shorthorns and free-range chickens and ducks - all reared exclusively for the George and Dragon and Askham Hall.

It has won many accolades including a Taste of England silver award (Visit Britain), Taste Cumbria (Cumbria Tourism) in 2011 and 2013 and highly commended in 2016, and Cumbria Life magazine Food and Drink awards 'Dining Pub of the Year' in 2014, as well as runner up in 2015 and 2016 and finalist in 2017.

The food, extensive wine list and selection of local ales are not the only things to impress. The thoughtfully designed interior is something to be admired too, with intimate alcoves with photographs and archive prints from the family estate. With a relaxed atmosphere, along with the wonderfully friendly staff who make you feel so welcome, you won't want to leave. And you don't have to - 11 beautifully and individually designed bedrooms mean the George and Dragon is also perfect for a holiday in a quiet and secluded part of Cumbria.

Executive chef Ian Jackson, together with his kitchen team are dedicated and passionate about using the best quality ingredients, much of which is grown and reared at its sister establishment, Askham Hall (page 46). The dishes shown have been prepared by Ian's senior chef Tim Kewley.

Forgotten your glasses?
Please borrow a pair.

CUMBERLAND SAUSAGE & BLACK PUDDING SCOTCH EGG, CRACKLING CRUST, PICCALILLI

SERVES 4

 Eden Gold, Golden Ale
(England)

Ingredients

Piccalilli (Makes more than required)
1 cauliflower (cut into small florets)
1 bulb fennel (finely chopped)
1 red chilli and 1 green chilli (finely sliced)
100g green beans (finely sliced)
3 banana shallots (finely chopped)
125g sea salt, ½ tsp mustard seeds
3 fresh bay leaves, ½ tsp pink peppercorns
100ml rapeseed oil
2 Bramley apples (grated)
330ml white wine vinegar
330g caster sugar
3 tsp English mustard powder
3 cloves garlic (crushed)
3 tsp turmeric
½ nutmeg (grated), 1 tsp ground cumin
100ml water
3 tbsp arrowroot

Eggs And Sausagemeat
4 medium free-range eggs
white wine vinegar (splash of)
1 banana shallot (finely diced)
½ tsp dry pennyroyal (can be substituted for dry thyme)
butter (knob of)
250g Cumberland sausagemeat
100g black pudding (finely diced)

Crackling Crust
100g Japanese panko breadcrumbs
1 pack pork scratchings
½ tsp onion powder, salt and pepper
seasoned flour and beaten egg (to *pane* Scotch eggs)

To Serve
sorrel, coriander, pork scratchings

Method

For The Piccalilli
Place the vegetables in a large colander in the sink and coat in the sea salt. Leave for 1½ hours until they have released some of their liquid and firmed up. Rinse off any excess salt.

Fry the mustard seeds, bay leaves and peppercorns in the oil in a large saucepan until the mustard seeds start to pop. Add the apples, vinegar, sugar and remaining spices and bring to the boil.

Combine the water and arrowroot, in a small bowl, then whisk into the hot mixture to form a thick paste. Add the vegetables to the pan and cook for 10-15 minutes until they start to release some of their juices. Store in sterilised Kilner jars.

> **Chef's Tip**
> Make the piccalilli well in advance and allow it to mature for a week in a sterilised Kilner jar so the flavours develop.

For The Eggs And Sausagemeat
Bring a pan of water to a rapid boil and add a splash of vinegar. Gently add the eggs and boil rapidly for 6 minutes and 15 seconds. Shock in iced water. Allow to cool, then peel.

Sweat the shallots and pennyroyal in the butter until translucent. Allow to cool, then combine with the Cumberland sausagemeat and diced black pudding.

Cling film a chopping board or kitchen surface. Divide the sausagemeat into 4, 90g balls.

Press the balls onto the cling film into rounds, just over 1cm thick. Place the soft-boiled eggs inside and wrap back into ball shapes around the egg.

For The Crackling Crust
Blend the breadcrumbs, scratchings, onion powder and seasoning to a coarse crumb in a food processor.

To Finish The Scotch Egg
Preheat the oven to 180°C (fan) and a deep fryer to 180°C.

To *pane* the Scotch eggs, roll them in flour, then beaten egg, then the crackling crust crumb.

Carefully fry the eggs for 2 minutes until golden all over. Transfer to an oven tray and bake for 8 minutes. Rest for 1 minute, then carve, serving with the piccalilli.

To Serve
Garnish with a little fresh sorrel, coriander and crushed scratchings. Blend some of the piccalilli into a purée to garnish the plate to add another texture.

HERDWICK HOGGET, BRAISED BARLEY, PARSLEY ROOT, GLAZED MUSHROOMS

SERVES 4

🍷 *Château Beaumont, Cru Bourgeois Supérieur 2005, Haut-Médoc, Bordeaux (France)*

Ingredients

Braised Belly
½ hogget belly (off the bone, trimmed, scored)
200g rock salt
1 sprig rosemary, 1 sprig thyme
100g celery (diced), 100g white onion (diced)
100g carrot (diced)
25g butter, 3 cloves garlic
3 bay leaves, 6 white peppercorns
500ml chicken stock
250ml red wine, 250ml white wine
salt (to season)

Braised Barley
250g pearl barley
500ml chicken stock, 100g butter
2 banana shallots (finely diced)
200g walnuts (toasted, rubbed and chopped)

Parsley Root Purée
175g parsley root (diced), 50g butter
250ml chicken stock
50ml double cream
salt and white pepper

Glazed Mushrooms
200g ceps or king oyster mushrooms
250ml chicken stock
150ml Eiswein vinegar (sherry or balsamic vinegar can be used instead)
25g caster sugar, 50g butter

Hogget
600g hogget loin (trimmed of all sinew and most fat)
vegetable oil (drizzle of)
50g salted butter
1 sprig thyme, sea salt

Garnish (optional)
Jerusalem artichokes (roasted)
baby red chard leaves

Method

For The Braised Belly (Allow 48 hours)
Place the belly in a large tray and rub well with the salt, rosemary and thyme. Cover with cling film and leave in the fridge for 3 hours (overnight is best).

Slowly caramelise the vegetables in the butter in a heavy-based saucepan and put to one side.

Preheat the oven to 140°C.

Brush any excess salt off the belly and place in a deep cooking dish. Add the vegetables, aromats, stock and wines. Cover with baking parchment and tin foil and braise in the oven for 4 hours.

Once cooled slightly, carefully remove the belly from the liquid, and press between 2 baking trays lined with baking parchment. Place a heavy pan on top, then transfer to the fridge. Press for a minimum of 2 hours (overnight is best). Pass the liquid through a *chinois* into a saucepan and reduce to sauce consistency, adjust the seasoning.

For The Braised Barley
Boil the barley in the chicken stock until tender, then set aside.

Sweat the shallots in half the butter, adding the chopped walnuts in at the last minute, toss together, then add to the barley.

Make a *beurre noisette* with the remaining butter, then stir into the barley. Set aside.

For The Parsley Root Purée
Sweat the parsley root in the butter, then add the chicken stock and simmer until soft. Pass the parsley root through a *chinois*, then blitz in a blender with the cream, adding chicken stock to adjust the consistency. Season.

For The Glazed Mushrooms
Reduce the stock, vinegar and sugar until syrupy for the glaze.

Halve the large wild mushrooms straight down the middle, then score the flat side. Pan fry in butter until tender. Add a tablespoon of the glaze mixture, basting continuously until fully glazed.

To Finish And Serve
Preheat the oven to 180°C (fan).

Lightly oil and season the hogget loin. Sear in a hot pan then turn down the heat and add the butter and thyme, basting the meat as you go. Slice the belly into portions and add to the pan, before transferring the whole pan to the oven, around 8 minutes for medium-rare. Remove from the oven and rest somewhere warm for 4 minutes before portioning.

Warm the barley with some of the sauce, garnish the plate with parsley root purée and glazed mushrooms; finish with as much of the belly braising *jus* as desired. Serve as pictured.

TREACLE TART, BROWN BUTTER ICE CREAM, LEMON BALM

SERVES 12

🍷 *Muscat de Beaumes de Venise, Domaine des Bernardins, 2006 (France)*

Ingredients

Tart Filling

125g salted butter
850g golden syrup
145ml double cream
2 large free-range eggs
2 egg yolks
1 tbsp sea salt
35g buckwheat flour
350g brown breadcrumbs

Sweet Pastry

50g caster sugar
1 large free-range egg
125g unsalted butter
200g plain flour

Brown Butter Ice Cream

60g light brown sugar
85g glucose
100ml water
300ml double cream
200ml whole milk
75g caster sugar
6 free-range egg yolks
sea salt (pinch of)
200g salted butter

Lemon Balm Gel

150g caster sugar
150g lemon balm
150ml water
1 lime (zest and juice of)
5g citric acid
agar agar (see method)

To Serve

fresh lemon balm
beurre noisette powder

23cm loose-bottomed tart case (greased)

Method

To Make The Tart Filling (Prepare ahead)
Brown the butter in a pan on a medium heat.
Warm the golden syrup in a separate pan. Pass the *beurre noisette* into the warm syrup and combine with a whisk.
Combine the cream, eggs and salt well, then whisk into the warm syrup and butter mix. Fold in the flour and breadcrumbs and leave the mixture to absorb the flavours overnight.

> **Chef's Tip**
> Make the filling the night before baking to allow the breadcrumbs to absorb the ingredients for a more even bake.

For The Sweet Pastry
Combine the sugar, egg and butter in a mixer. Fold in the flour to form a dough. Wrap in cling film and rest in the fridge for 30 minutes.
Preheat the oven to 180°C (fan).
Roll the pastry to ½cm thickness on a lightly floured worktop. Carefully transfer to the prepared tart case, leaving the overhang untrimmed. Prick with a fork and blind bake for 12 minutes.
Reduce the oven to 160°C (fan).
Fill the baked tart case to the top with the filling. Bake for 20 minutes, then lower the temperature to 140°C (fan) and bake for a further 30 minutes. Allow to cool.

For The Brown Butter Ice Cream (Prepare ahead)
Put the brown sugar, glucose and water into a heavy-based saucepan and bring to a golden caramel. Add 50ml of the double cream at the end to stop the cooking process.
Without boiling, warm the remaining cream and milk together. Whisk the sugar and yolks until pale. Pour the milk mix over the yolks, whisk together with a pinch of salt, then return to the pan. Heat gently until the custard coats the back of a spoon. Cool.
Make a *beurre noisette* by gently heating the butter until it browns. Pass through a *chinois* and set aside somewhere warm.
Combine the caramel and custard in a blender, slowly adding the *beurre noisette*. Once cool, churn in an ice cream machine.

For The Lemon Balm Gel
Bring all the ingredients, apart from the agar agar, to the boil. When it becomes a light syrup, pass through a *chinois*. Measure the liquid, then return to a pan. Add 1g of agar agar for every 100ml of liquid, boil for a few minutes until it starts to thicken, then pour into a plastic tub and set in the fridge. Once set, cut the jelly into cubes and blitz in a blender until smooth.

To Serve
Serve as pictured.

THE GOLDEN FLEECE

Ruleholme, Irthington, Carlisle, Cumbria, CA6 4NF

01228 573 686
www.thegoldenfleececumbria.co.uk Twitter: @fleeceruleholme Facebook: The Golden Fleece Cumbria

Nestled in rolling north Cumbrian countryside, The Golden Fleece Inn and Restaurant is just a stone's throw from iconic Hadrian's Wall. Within easy reach of the Lake District and only a few miles from the historic city of Carlisle and the picturesque market town of Brampton, 'The Fleece' is a popular haven for locals, walkers and visitors to the area.

Owners Robert and Sylvia Cowan began a sympathetic refurbishment of the traditional country inn when they purchased it in 2011, with a clear vision of what they wanted to achieve. With great attention to detail, they created a relaxed and welcoming ambience for their guests, with open fires for the winter months and lovely garden areas to sit out, eat and play when the weather is kind.

They are inspired to offer not only good food, but something a little unusual - something a bit exceptional. Quality ingredients are prepared with care and presented with professional flair and imagination. The menu changes with the seasons and is predominantly from local produce, with all the meat coming from local farms.

And whilst the food is important, it's only part of the package that Robert and Sylvia take care to provide. Friendly, attentive staff will always ensure that guests enjoy the whole eating out experience, and are made to feel special.

Robert heads up the kitchen team where he continues to pursue his successful vision, winning several local awards as well as an AA Rosette and inclusion in the Michelin Guide.

Cadrian Suite

TWICE BAKED THREE CHEESE SOUFFLE

SERVES 4

Domaine de Cibadies, Chardonnay
(France)

Ingredients

Soufflé

30g butter
30g plain flour
150ml semi-skimmed milk
150ml double cream
30g smoked cheddar (finely grated)
30g hard white cheese (finely grated)
1 dtsp English mustard
salt and pepper
3 medium eggs (separated)

Topping

30g hard white cheese (finely grated)
100ml double cream

To Prepare The Moulds

4 soufflé moulds
30g butter (softened)
30g Parmesan (finely grated)

To Serve

seasonal salad leaves (dressed)

Method

For The Soufflé

Prepare the soufflé moulds by brushing them with the softened butter. Finish with brush strokes upwards, dust with the finely grated Parmesan and place in the fridge to chill.

Melt the butter in a saucepan, add the flour and cook through until the mixture becomes slightly pale. Gradually add the milk and cream, stirring continuously. Bring to a simmer, add the rest of the grated cheeses, the mustard and seasoning and leave to cool slightly before beating in the egg yolks.

Whisk the egg whites to stiff peaks and fold into the cheese mixture. Pour the mixture into the prepared moulds.

Preheat the oven to 180°C (fan).

Place the moulds in an ovenproof dish, then half fill the dish with water to make a *bain-marie*. Bake in the oven for 35 minutes. Remove the soufflés from the *bain-marie* and set aside to cool. They will have risen above the moulds and will drop whilst cooling.

Chef's Tip

The soufflés are best made the day before.

To Serve

Preheat the oven to 200°C (fan).

Turn out the soufflés from their moulds and place in an ovenproof dish. Pour a generous amount of cream over and sprinkle with the grated cheese. Bake for 7 minutes and serve immediately with a dressed side salad.

ROAST BEST END OF LAMB, BRAISED SHOULDER, ROSEMARY JUS, GOAT'S CHEESE CROQUETTE

SERVES 4

 Kangarilla Road, Shiraz (Australia)

Ingredients

Braised Lamb Shoulder

15g each carrots, onion and leeks (chopped)
500g lamb shoulder
salt and pepper
pig's caul
50g dates (chopped)

Cannons Of Lamb

4 x 125g prepared cannons of lamb
fresh mint and parsley (few sprigs of, chopped)
2 cloves garlic (crushed)
olive oil (to cover)

Goat's Cheese Croquettes

500g potatoes
butter (large knob of)
cream (to bind)
100g goat's cheese (grated)
plain flour
1 egg (beaten)
panko breadcrumbs
vegetable oil (to deep fry)

Rosemary Jus

15g each carrots, onion and leeks (chopped)
butter (knob of)
500ml chicken stock
150ml port
3 tsp redcurrant jelly
1 sprig rosemary

To Serve

tender-stem broccoli

Method

For The Braised Lamb Shoulder (Prepare the day before)

Preheat the oven to 125ºC (fan).

Place the chopped vegetables in an ovenproof dish with the shoulder on top. Season and pour on a little water. Cover tightly with foil and place in the oven for 4 hours or until the meat easily falls apart.

Remove from the oven and allow to cool until you can handle the meat. Pull the meat apart, remove any excessive fat and place in a bowl. Add the dates and enough of the cooking *liquor* to make a moist mix. Place in the fridge to cool.

For The Cannons Of Lamb (Prepare the day before)

Place the lamb cannons in a bowl with the chopped herbs and the garlic with enough olive oil to cover.

Cover tightly with cling film and place in the fridge overnight to marinate.

For The Goat's Cheese Croquettes

Boil the potatoes until soft, mash, season and add butter and cream. Stir in the goat's cheese and mix well. Allow to cool slightly, then place in a piping bag and pipe into long sausages. Cut into 35mm pieces and set aside to cool. Roll in the flour, egg and breadcrumbs. Fry in hot oil until golden.

For The Rosemary Jus

Sauté the vegetables in the butter for 5 minutes until soft. Add the chicken stock, port, redcurrant jelly and rosemary. Reduce until a syrup-like consistency is achieved, then pass through a fine sieve.

To Finish And Serve

Preheat the oven to 200ºC (fan).

Divide the shoulder mix into 125g balls. Wrap in the pig's caul and flatten. Seal in a hot pan and place in the hot oven to finish for 10 minutes.

Remove the lamb cannons from the marinade and seal in a hot pan. Finish in the oven, 7 minutes for medium rare. Allow to rest for 5 minutes before serving.

Slice the cannons and assemble with the shoulder and croquettes as pictured. Spoon a little of the concentrated jus around and serve with tender-stem broccoli.

Chef's Tip

You can prepare all the elements of this dish ahead of time.

POOR KNIGHTS' PUDDING

SERVES 4

🍷 *The Ned, Noble Sauvignon Blanc
(New Zealand)*

Method

For The Pudding

Boil the milk and cream with the vanilla pod. Leave to cool slightly for the vanilla to infuse, then slice the pod and scrape out the seeds. Return the seeds to the mix and discard the pod. Pour the hot milk and cream mix over the beaten eggs and caster sugar and mix well.

Slice the croissants in half horizontally, spread with the marmalade and fill with the slices of apple. Arrange in an ovenproof dish just large enough for a snug fit. Pour over the custard mix and leave for 15 minutes to absorb into the croissants. Sprinkle over the Demerara sugar and cover tightly with foil.

Preheat the oven to 115°C (fan).

Place the dish in a *bain-marie* and bake in the oven for 35 minutes, or until the custard has set.

To Serve

Serve with good quality vanilla bean ice cream.

Chef's Tip

This dish came about from a little story we were told. In days of old when our knights went to fight in the Crusades, on their return they found their castles and estates had been plundered. All they had left were the apples from the orchards, a little wheat to make some bread and milk from the cow. They managed to make their version of 'poor knights' 'pudding'; ours is a little more indulgent.

Ingredients

Pudding

125ml semi-skimmed milk
125ml double cream
1 vanilla pod
4 medium eggs (beaten)
50g caster sugar
4 baked croissants
1 tbsp marmalade
1 eating apple (peeled, cored, sliced)
2 tbsp Demerara sugar

To Serve

good quality vanilla bean ice cream

136
HARE & HOUNDS

Levens, Kendal, Cumbria, LA8 8PN

015395 60004
www.hareandhoundslevens.co.uk Twitter: @handhlevens Facebook: Hare and Hounds, Levens

The Hare and Hounds is a glorious 16th Century coaching inn set in the pretty village of Levens, in the Lyth Valley, perfectly placed for replenishment after a day out exploring the fells and lakes. After completing refurbishments in 2015, it has four fabulous bedrooms and The Barn, a new dining experience, all in keeping with the character of this remarkable building.

Owned and run by Becky and Ash Dewar since 2013, it's a proper village pub, full of character and thoughtful touches. Becky and Ash enjoy welcoming their guests with a mean cocktail list, local cask ales, great craft beers and delicious comfort food with a twist.

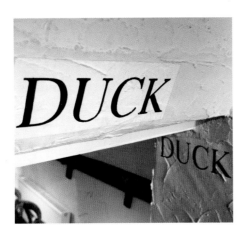

Food at the Hare and Hounds is simple, fresh and tasty. Home cooked, hearty dishes both new and traditional with big flavours and perfect balance. Hand-rolled-to-order pizzas, seasonal specials and its renowned burgers all feature on the menu. All its food is locally sourced and made from scratch by head chef Allan Kay and his team, supported by sous chef Will.

Love and care are poured into every dish and the result is that each is beautifully presented, wholesome and satisfying. The small and passionate team at the Hare and Hounds pride themselves on their friendly and knowledgeable service.

The Hare and Hounds welcomes everyone - kids, muddy boots and dogs included.

The fans of the Hare and Hounds come back again and again for its seriously tasty food, guaranteed friendly welcome, and a truly fun and relaxing time.

FLAKED NATURALLY SMOKED HADDOCK, CRISPY EGG, CURRIED MAYONNAISE

SERVES 4

 Swan Blonde, Bowness Bay Brewery, Kendal (England)

Ingredients

Haddock

milk (splash of)
1 large, naturally smoked haddock fillet (skinned, pin boned)
1 spring onion (finely sliced)
1 tbsp coriander leaves (chopped)

Curry Paste

100ml white wine
1 tsp turmeric
3 tsp mild Madras curry powder
1 tsp cumin
1 tsp ground coriander
40g onion (finely chopped)
1 clove garlic (finely chopped)

Mayonnaise

2 egg yolks
10g Dijon mustard
10ml white wine vinegar
400ml vegetable oil
lemon juice and salt (to season)

Crispy Egg

6 eggs
milk (splash of)
100g plain flour
100g panko breadcrumbs
oil (for deep frying)

To Serve

tomato wedges
roquito pearl chilli peppers
micro coriander
red amaranth
curly endive

Method

For The Haddock

Bring a pan of water to the boil and add a splash of milk. Turn the water down to a simmer and add the fish, cook for 4-5 minutes. Drain the fish into a sieve and leave to cool.

For The Curry Paste

Pour the wine into a saucepan and mix in the dry ingredients. Add the onion and garlic and reduce slowly on the stove until it becomes a thick paste. Leave to cool.

For The Curried Mayonnaise

Place the egg yolks, mustard and vinegar into a bowl. Bind the ingredients together using a balloon whisk, then add a very small amount of the oil and whisk until it is well blended. Keep adding a little more oil whilst whisking. Continue until it *emulsifies* and stop adding oil when it reaches a very thick consistency. Stir in the curry paste and season to taste using the lemon juice and salt.

Chef's Tip

If you don't like curry flavour, this dish is equally nice with grain mustard mayonnaise.

For The Crispy Egg

Fill a bowl with cold water and ice cubes.

Bring a saucepan of water to the boil and add 4 of the eggs. Set a timer for 6 minutes 30 seconds. When the timer goes off, remove the eggs and immediately place them in the iced water. Once cooled, carefully peel the eggs, and drain well.

Beat the remaining eggs with a splash of milk in a bowl. Place the flour and breadcrumbs in 2 separate bowls. Coat each boiled egg in flour, then egg wash and finally the breadcrumbs. Deep fry the coated eggs at 180°C for 45 seconds.

To Assemble The dish

Gently flake the cooked haddock and combine with the spring onion and coriander. Fold in the curried mayonnaise making sure it has a stiff texture. Place the crispy egg on top and serve immediately.

MAPLE CURED GAMMON RIBEYE, CRUSHED NEW POTATOES, ROAST CELERIAC, SAVOY CABBAGE, BEETROOT, ROSEMARY ONION JUS

SERVES 4

 Château Bernateau, Saint-Emilion Grand Cru, Bordeaux (France)

Ingredients

4 x 285g maple cured gammon ribeye steaks

Crushed New Potatoes

600g new potatoes
butter (knob of)

Savoy Cabbage

1 onion (finely diced)
150ml white wine
250ml double cream
2 tsp cornflour and water paste
1 tbsp Parmesan (grated)
½ Savoy cabbage (finely shredded)

Beetroot

2 golden beetroot
2 purple beetroot

Celeriac

25ml vegetable oil
1 small celeriac (peeled)

Rosemary Onion Jus

25ml vegetable oil
150g silverskin onions (frozen)
150ml red wine
1 tsp rosemary (finely chopped)
750ml beef stock (reduced to 250ml)
salt and pepper

Method

For The Crushed New Potatoes

Place the potatoes in a pan of cold, salted water and bring to the boil. Simmer for 20 minutes or until cooked. Drain well, season and crush with a knob of butter.

For The Savoy Cabbage

Add the onion to the wine and reduce to a syrup. Add the cream, season and thicken with the cornflour paste. Stir the Parmesan into the sauce when thick.

Blanch the shredded cabbage in a pan of boiling water for 30 seconds, drain well, then stir into the wine sauce.

For The Beetroot

Boil the beetroots separately until they are cooked through. Cool in iced water, then peel and cut into neat wedges.

For The Celeriac

Preheat the oven to 200°C (fan).

Heat a roasting tray with oil in the oven. Cut the celeriac into neat batons, place on the tray and roast until golden brown, about 20 minutes.

For The Rosemary Onion Jus

Heat a pan with the vegetable oil until it is extremely hot. Add the frozen onions, stir until golden brown, then drain and set aside. Add the red wine to the same pan, reduce slightly, add the rosemary and the reserved onions. Pour in the beef stock to make a sauce consistency. Season to taste.

For The Gammon Ribeye

Preheat the oven to 200°C (fan).

Brush the gammon steaks with oil and season. Mark them on the chargrill with a crisscross pattern, giving 1 minute for each set of markings. Finish the steaks off on a tray in the oven for 6-8 minutes.

To Serve

Ensure all elements of the dish are hot and plate as pictured.

> **Chef's Tip**
> This dish is equally as nice with game or chicken.

PASSION FRUIT PANNA COTTA, CHOCOLATE CHUNKS, CARAMÉLISED PINEAPPLE, CHILLI LIME SYRUP

SERVES 4

 Local Damson Gin and Fever-Tree Elderflower Tonic. Damson gin from Strawberry Bank Liqueurs, Lyth Valley (England)

Ingredients

Passion Fruit Panna Cotta

300ml double cream
150g passion fruit purée
50g caster sugar
1¾ leaves gelatine (soaked in cold water)

Brownie

200g dark chocolate
160g unsalted butter
3 large eggs
150g caster sugar
40g plain flour

Chilli Lime Syrup

2 limes (juice and zest of)
100g golden caster sugar
2 red chillies (finely diced)

Caramelised Pineapple

1 pineapple
25g butter
1 tbsp Demerara sugar

Garnish

edible flowers

4 x 170g aluminium pudding moulds
20cm x 17cm baking tray (lined with parchment)

Method

For The Passion Fruit Panna Cotta (Prepare ahead)

Heat the cream, passion fruit purée and sugar in a pan until hot but not boiling. Squeeze any excess water from the gelatine, then stir into the warm mixture. Pass the mix through a sieve into the moulds and refrigerate overnight.

For The Brownie

Preheat the oven to 180°C (fan).

Melt the chocolate and butter together. While they melt, whisk the eggs and sugar together until light in colour, then combine with the melted butter and chocolate. Sift in the flour and pour the mixture into the prepared tin. Bake for 30 minutes until set and slightly cracked.

For The Chilli Lime Syrup

Add water to the lime juice to make it up to 150ml. Place the zest, sugar, chillies and lime juice mix in a pan and boil for 10 minutes until thick.

For The Caramelised Pineapple

Using an apple corer, make 20 pineapple cylinders. Warm the butter in a pan until it begins to sizzle, then mix in the Demerara sugar and stir until it has melted. Roll the pineapple cylinders in the mixture and drain.

To Assemble

Remove the panna cottas from the fridge and serve, as pictured, with all the other elements at room temperature.

> **Chef's Tip**
>
> For an easy way to unmould the panna cotta, simply run under a hot water tap for 3 seconds and it should slide out.

146
HOLBECK GHYLL

Holbeck Lane, Windermere, Cumbria, LA23 1LU

015394 32375
www.holbeckghyll.com

With a magnificent view of Lake Windermere and the Langdale Fells, Holbeck Ghyll is idyllic in any season, surrounded by the natural beauty of Cumbria. Its renowned restaurant overlooks lakes and mountains. Built in the 19th Century, the house was bought as a hunting lodge in 1888 by Lord Lonsdale, then one of the richest men in the country, whose name went down in history when he bequeathed the Lonsdale Belt to boxing.

The Oak Room restaurant overlooks lake and mountains, as do many bedrooms in the main house and the nearby lodge. Some of the spacious suites have been designed for families, while the luxurious Miss Potter Suite is perfect for that romantic special occasion - a detached suite with a private terrace and hot tub.

Relaxation at Holbeck Ghyll can take the form of walking or boating, golf or bird watching... or indulging in a range of facilities and treatments available at the spa and in its newly launched bar, restaurant and state of the art kitchen which provides a table next to the chef's pass.

Holbeck Ghyll is proud to introduce you to Jake Jones, its new head chef and one of Britain's fastest rising young talents. At 26 years old Jake has already proved himself in some of the country's most demanding kitchens, developing his skills alongside some of the nation's top chefs. Jake has a unique style and direction, drawing on his experiences, offering something new and exciting, delivered with incredible passion and ambition.

Under Jake's direction, there is no doubt that the famous kitchen and its excellent reputation is in very safe hands.

The captivating view of the Central Fells and Lake Windermere has been voted as one of the top 15 views in the world. Combined with style and comfort, Holbeck Ghyll offers a truly unique experience.

FERMENTED BARLEY 'PORRIDGE', RAMSONS, PERIGORD TRUFFLE, ASPARAGUS

SERVES 4

🍷 *Amalaya Torrontés/Riesling Calchaquí Valley,*
Salta, 2015 (Argentina)
Citrus and grapefruit notes from the Torrontés are
tempered by the elegant Riesling.

Ingredients

Fermented Barley Porridge

500g pearl barley
250ml live buttermilk
2 litres water
500ml white chicken stock (plus extra to loosen)
100g sheep's yoghurt
50g butter
10 asparagus spears
oil (drizzle of)
150g Berkswell sheep's cheese (grated)
salt (pinch of)
1 lemon (juice of, to taste)

Puffed Pearl Barley

50g pearl barley
250ml beef stock
vegetable oil (to fry)
salt

Garnish

16 wild garlic shoots
wild garlic flowers
Perigord truffle (finely shaved)
50ml ramsons (wild garlic) oil

Method

For The Fermented Barley Porridge (Prepare ahead)

Ferment the pearl barley by covering it with water, adding the live buttermilk and leaving it at room temperature for 1 day.

Drain the barley from the water and buttermilk, keep the liquid.

Add the barley to a pan with the chicken stock and some of the fermenting *liquor* to just cover. Simmer for around 15 minutes until just cooked, remove from the liquid and spread on a tray. Chill.

Add the barley to a pan, add the sheep's yoghurt, butter and some more chicken stock, warm slowly.

Whilst this is warming, peel the asparagus, remove about 2½cm from the top of the asparagus and slice in half. Roast the tips in a pan of oil until dark golden brown. Slice the rest of the asparagus thinly.

Add the grated cheese, salt and lemon juice to the pearl barley, it should have the consistency of risotto, then add the sliced asparagus and fold through.

For The Puffed Pearl Barley

Cook the pearl barley in the beef stock until tender, about 30 minutes. Spread on a non-stick mat and dry in the oven at 60°C for 5-6 hours. Heat the vegetable oil to 200°C and drop in the dried barley until it puffs up. Drain and season with salt.

To Serve

Spoon the pearl barley into a bowl, add the charred asparagus, spoon on top a little of the puffed pearl barley and drizzle a little wild garlic oil. Place the wild garlic shoots and flowers on, then grate on the black truffle with a microplane.

Chef's Tip

This dish is the second course on our tasting menu; you could increase the portion size and add wild mushrooms for a normal starter size.

BELTED GALLOWAY, SALSIFY, BITTER LEAVES, MISO

SERVES 4

🍷 *Casa Silva Carmenere Los Lingues, Colchagua, 2014 (Chile)*

Ingredients

Beef Jus
1½ litres beef stock, 1 sprig thyme

Jacob's Ladder
2kg piece of Jacob's ladder
brine (15% salt/85% water)
150ml beef stock
2 sprigs thyme, 2 cloves garlic
200ml beef jus

Miso Butter
100g butter
40g white miso paste
25ml beef jus, salt (pinch of)

Beef Butter
100g Cumbrian butter
5g Marmite, 35ml beef jus
1g salt, 8g white miso paste

Salsify
500g salsify
1 lemon (juice of), water (to cover)
beef butter (see above)
1 sprig thyme, 1 clove garlic

Mushrooms
16 Blewit mushrooms
rice wine vinegar (splash of)
butter (2 knobs of), 1 head red chicory
1 head chicory, endive (picked)

Beef Fillet
4 x 170g belted Galloway beef fillet steaks
(room temperature)
butter (knob of)
Maldon sea salt (sprinkle of)

To Serve
250g smoked bone marrow (sliced)

Method

For The Beef Jus
Add the sprig of thyme to the stock and reduce down to 300ml. Pass through a muslin cloth 3 times.

For The Jacob's Ladder (Allow 72 hours)
Brine the Jacob's ladder for 24 hours. Wash and dry, vac pack with the beef stock, thyme and garlic and cook at 85°C for 24 hours. Take out of the bag and remove the bones and the tough top layer of meat, leaving the tender underneath layer. Cover with greaseproof paper, place a heavy weight on top of the meat and press for 12 hours.
Once pressed, dice into 2cm cubes. Warm and glaze in beef jus to serve.

For The Miso Butter
Mix the butter with the miso paste, salt and the beef jus.

For The Beef Butter
Combine all the ingredients and store in the fridge.

For The Salsify
Peel the salsify and immediately place in an acid bath of lemon and water. Once all are peeled, vac pack with the beef butter, thyme and garlic and cook at 83°C for 1 hour. Plunge into ice water, remove from the bags and cut into equal sized pieces. Colour the salsify in a pan until golden brown, finish by brushing with miso butter.

For The Beef Fillet
Colour the fillets in a hot pan, then add the butter and baste until the desired cook is reached, ideally medium rare, then rest.

> **Chef's Tip**
> Always choose beef that has been aged for at least 35 days. It makes a huge difference in flavour.

For The Mushrooms, Chicory And Endive
Pan fry the mushrooms, then finish with rice wine vinegar and butter to glaze.
Cook the endive in butter.
Carefully break down the chicory to separate leaves.

To Serve
Slice the beef fillet and brush with miso butter. Season with Maldon sea salt.
Plate alongside the glazed short rib in the jus. Place the salsify on the plate and arrange the mushrooms on top, followed by the bitter leaves. Blow torch the smoked bone marrow slices and place between the leaves. Finish by spooning on the beef jus.

CHOCOLATE, WHIPPED CHEESE, BEETROOT

SERVES 4

🍷 *Maury Solera 1928, Les Vignerons de Maury,*
(France)
Hand harvested with no fining or filteration, this
sweet wine is made in the solera system, similar
to sherry. Intense and deeply coloured, beautiful
with chocolate.

Ingredients

Chocolate Mousse

220g bitter chocolate
2 egg yolks
80ml double cream (boiled)
280ml double cream (whipped)

Beetroot Meringues

100ml beetroot juice
100g dried egg white powder
120g sugar
beetroot powder (to dust)

Whipped Cheese

100g cream cheese
100g Yellison Farm crowdie
80g icing sugar
1 orange (zest of)
1 vanilla pod (scraped)

Beetroot Discs

400ml beetroot juice
180g sugar
2 large beetroot

To Finish

beetroot powder (to dust)
micro red amaranth

Method

For The Chocolate Mousse

Melt the chocolate, beat in the egg yolks and pour over the
boiled double cream. Fold in the whipped cream. Transfer to a
plastic container and store in the fridge.

For The Beetroot Meringues (Prepare ahead)

Whisk the egg white powder with the beetroot juice until
aerated. Gradually add the sugar whilst whisking until glossy,
pipe onto trays, dust with beetroot powder and dry in the oven
at 60°C for 6-8 hours.

For The Whipped Cheese

Add the cream cheese, crowdie, sugar, orange zest and vanilla
pod to a KitchenAid and whip for 3-4 minutes until thick
and glossy.

For The Beetroot Discs

Boil the beetroot juice and sugar and reduce by half. Slice the
beetroot on a mandoline and cut out with a 10mm round cutter.
Place into a container and pour over the hot syrup. Set aside
to cool.

To Serve

Place a *quenelle* of chocolate mousse on the plate, pipe the
crowdie cream around and place on the beetroot discs.
Finish with the meringues, a dusting of beetroot powder and
micro amaranth.

156
HRISHI AT GILPIN

Gilpin Hotel & Lake House, Crook Road, Windermere, The Lake District, LA23 3NE

015394 88818
www.thegilpin.co.uk Twitter: @gilpinhotel

At the heart of Gilpin is a very passionate family and team, dedicated to creating lasting memories for their guests who return time and again for celebrations and escapes. With 5 stars, one Michelin Star and three AA Rosettes, warmth and friendliness are balanced with extraordinary service, exquisite décor and stunning culinary experiences at these two luxury country houses spanning two estates in the beautiful Lake District.

Dine in either the Michelin starred main restaurant, 'Hrishi', where Hrishikesh Desai combines great Lake District produce and classic methods to deliver unbelievable textures and flavours with just a twist of Asia, or in 'Gilpin Spice', an informal restaurant transcending international boundaries, with an open kitchen focussing on dishes from the spice trail spanning the Indian sub-continent, Malaysia, Thailand, Indonesia, the Philippines, Japan and China.

At Gilpin Hotel, all the bedrooms have lovely Lakeland views, most leading directly onto the gardens - six Garden Suites with their own cedarwood hot tubs, and five fabulous detached Spa Lodges with private en suite spas (rainmaker showers and steam rooms inside, hydrotherapy hot tubs and saunas outside) for a very special, private experience. Only a mile away at Gilpin Lake House, just six suites enjoy exclusive access to 100 acres of grounds, including a stunningly beautiful private lake, boathouse, pool, hot tubs and spa.

Photography by André Ainsworth, Tony West & Ben Barden

n Lake House

Gilpin Hotel

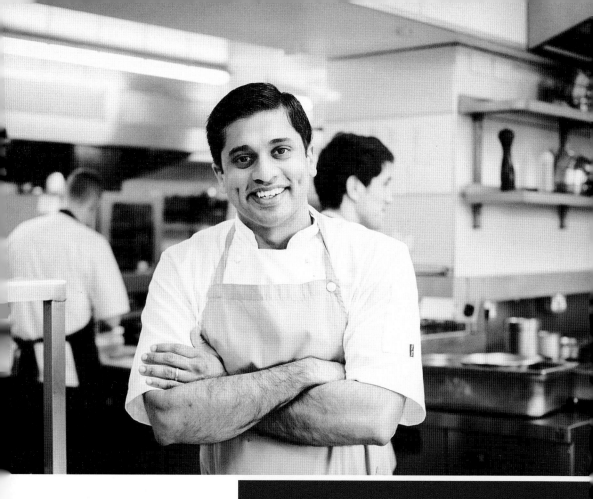

The spirit of Gilpin is motivated by love and laughter - our guests', and ours. We hope to see you soon in the beautiful Lake District.

SCALLOP CEVICHE, CARROT & CUMIN PUREE

SERVES 4

 Muscadet de Sèvre-et-Maine 'Sur Lie' 2013
Château de Chasseloir (France)

Ingredients

8 scallops

Carrot & Cumin Purée

1g whole cumin seeds
50g butter
500g carrots (peeled, diced)
salt and pepper
100ml water
olive oil

Ceviche Dressing

120ml fresh orange juice
200ml orange juice (reduced to 50ml)
15ml lemon juice
30ml sherry vinegar
30ml sunflower oil
10g fresh ginger (finely diced)
2 red chillies (finely chopped)
1 sprig mint (leaves of)

Garnish

rock salt
24 green apple batons
15g black tobiko caviar
12 toasted hazelnuts (halved)
herbs (fennel cress and red amaranth or coriander cress)

Method

For The Carrot & Cumin Purée (Makes more than required)

Fry the cumin seeds in foaming butter on a high heat until golden. Add the carrots, season and sweat for 6 minutes. Pour in the water, cover with cling film and cook until tender. Blend until smooth adding some olive oil to *emulsify*. Pour the liquid into a squeezy bottle.

For The Ceviche Dressing (Prepare ahead, makes more than required)

Mix all the ingredients together. Leave for 24 hours in the fridge, then drain, separating out the ginger and chilli to use as the garnish. Pour the liquid into a squeezy bottle.

Chef's Tip

The ceviche dressing can be used with different salads, such as tuna or fennel, or drizzle over pizzas. It will stay fresh in the fridge for 1 week.

For The Scallops

Thinly slice the scallops and store in the fridge until ready to use.

To Serve

Lay the scallop slices in a circle on 4 plates and sprinkle with rock salt. Arrange the apple batons, 5 dots of carrot purée, 3 small piles of the ginger and chilli (saved from the ceviche dressing) and caviar onto the scallops. Garnish with the hazelnuts and herbs. Just before serving, finish with the ceviche dressing.

LOIN OF SPRING LAMB, MASALA SAUCE, PEA PUREE

SERVES 4

🍷 *Rioja Crianza 2013 Bodegas Sierra Cantabria (Spain)*

Ingredients

Potato Terrine
2kg Redskin potatoes (peeled, thinly sliced)
100g butter
2 cloves garlic (crushed), 8 sprigs thyme, salt

Red Onion Marmalade
1kg medium-sized red onions (finely diced)
50ml vegetable oil, rock salt (sprinkle of)
20ml balsamic vinegar, salt and sugar (to taste)

Lamb Jus
500ml lamb stock, 250ml chicken stock
250ml beef stock, 125ml Madeira (reduced to 40ml)

Lamb Neck
2 lamb neck fillets, 1 head garlic (cut in half)
1 sprig rosemary, 1 sprig thyme
¼ of the red onion marmalade, salt and pepper
14 basil leaves (*julienne*), lamb jus (to moisten)
12 slices pancetta, flour (to dust)
emulsion (100ml water, 50g butter, salt)

Masala Sauce
125g onions (chopped), 30g desiccated coconut
8g black sesame seeds, 8g ground cumin
3 cloves garlic, 7g fresh ginger, ⅓ bunch coriander
75ml water, 500g chopped tomatoes (blended, sieved),
50ml vegetable oil, 8g garam masala
salt, sugar, lemon juice (to taste)

Lamb Loin
300g lamb loin (seasoned), olive oil (drizzle of)
butter (knob of), 1 sprig thyme, 1 clove garlic (crushed)

Baby Aubergines
2 baby aubergines (cut lengthways), salt, olive oil

Pea Purée
½ onion (finely chopped), 40g butter
500g defrosted peas, water, ½ bag spinach`
salt and sugar (to season), 20g cold butter (diced)

Scorched Cucumber
½ cucumber (seeds removed, cut into batons)
olive oil (drizzle of), salt (to season)

To Serve
100g spinach (wilted), micro coriander
8 baby asparagus tips (cooked with butter)

Method

For The Potato Terrine (Prepare ahead)
Preheat the oven to 180°C (fan).
Melt the butter, garlic and thyme in a pan. Layer the potato in a lined gastro or terrine mould, brushing each layer with the garlic, butter and salt. When 3cm deep, top with greaseproof paper and another gastro, cook for 40 minutes. Press, weighted, in the fridge for 8 hours. Cut into portions. Brown and warm in a non-stick pan.

For The Red Onion Marmalade
Cook the onions in the oil and rock salt until caramelised. Add the vinegar and reduce. Season to taste.

For The Lamb Jus
Reduce the stocks to a sauce consistency, then stir in the Madeira. Reduce to a jus.

For The Lamb Neck (Prepare ahead)
Preheat the oven to 130°C (fan).
Sear the fillets until golden. Add the garlic and herbs and cover with foil. Cook in the oven for 6 hours. Cool, then pick the meat into small strips. Add the onion marmalade and season. Stir in the basil and a little lamb jus. Wrap in cling film, roll in a sausage shape and chill. Portion, wrap in pancetta, dust with flour and sear. Heat in the oven with the *emulsion* and glaze with lamb jus.

For The Masala Sauce
Blitz the onions, coconut, sesame seeds, cumin, garlic, ginger, coriander and water. Fry in oil until golden. Add the tomatoes, cover and cook for 2 hours. Add the garam masala. Season.

For The Lamb Loin
Preheat the oven to 180°C (fan).
Sear the loin in the oil. Roast in the oven for 15 minutes. Add the butter, thyme and garlic and baste. Rest, then cut into 4.

For The Baby Aubergines
Preheat the oven to 180°C (fan).
Score the aubergine flesh. Season with salt and oil. Place the 2 halves together, wrap in foil and cook for 15 minutes. Remove the foil, place flesh-side up and top neatly with the masala sauce.

For The Pea Purée
Fry the onion in the butter, add the peas and stir. Cover with water and boil for 3 minutes. Add the spinach, season and blend until smooth. *Emulsify* with the butter and pass through a *chinois*.

For The Scorched Cucumber
Vac pack the cucumber and oil for 2 hours. Season and scorch with a blow torch.

To Serve
Serve as pictured with the lamb jus drizzled around the dish.

PEANUT BUTTER SEMIFREDDO, BANANA ICE CREAM

SERVES 4

🍷 *Maury Rouge 2014 Domaine Maury Doré (France)*

Ingredients

Peanut Butter Semifreddo

3 egg yolks
35g caster sugar
15ml water
45g smooth peanut butter
1 vanilla pod (seeds of)
100ml double cream (whipped to a one string consistency)

Banana Ice Cream

250ml whole milk
250ml double cream
110g caster sugar
6 egg yolks
125g banana purée (bought in frozen, defrosted)

Chocolate Fudge Sauce

60g dark chocolate
30g butter
30g golden syrup
120g dark soft brown sugar
180ml double cream
1 vanilla pod (scraped)

Candied Peanuts

125g raw peanuts
50g sugar
15ml water

Caramelised Banana

1 whole banana (skin removed, cut into 4)
40g Demerara sugar

Chef's Tip

The sauce for this dish goes perfectly well with sticky toffee pudding!

Method

For The Peanut Butter Semifreddo (Prepare ahead)

Place the yolks and 5g of the sugar in a mixing bowl and start whisking to form a peak consistency. You can use a hand held electric whisk or a Kitchen Aid.

Heat the remaining sugar and water up to 117°C, pour over the yolks and increase the speed. Whisk the *sabayon* until warm.

Beat the peanut butter and vanilla seeds in a large bowl until smooth. Fold in half of the *sabayon* mix and beat. Fold in the remaining *sabayon*, then the cream and freeze into your desired shape/mould.

For The Banana Ice Cream (Prepare ahead)

Heat the milk and cream in a pan and bring to the boil.

Whisk the sugar and yolks together. As soon as the cream is boiling, add half of it to the yolk mixture and whisk together well, then add back to the remaining cream in the pan.

Turn the heat down low and, using a wooden spoon, start stirring until the temperature reaches 84°C or the custard coats the back of the spoon. Remove from the heat immediately, add the banana purée and whisk. Pass through a fine sieve and allow to cool. Churn in an ice cream machine and freeze.

For The Chocolate Fudge Sauce

Slowly melt the chocolate, butter and syrup together in a heavy-based pan over a low heat being careful not to burn or crystallise the chocolate.

Separately, heat the sugar, cream and vanilla seeds. Bring to the boil whisking constantly, then pass through a fine sieve over the hot, melted chocolate. Whisk well and keep hot.

For The Candied Peanuts

Preheat the oven to 180°C.

Roast the peanuts for about 6-8 minutes or until golden, leave to cool.

Bring the sugar and water to the boil and cook to 130°C. Tip in the cold peanuts and keep stirring until the sugar crystallises. Spread evenly on trays. Once cool, keep in airtight tubs. This can be a cool snack as well.

For The Caramelised Banana

Dip one side of the banana in the Demerara sugar. Shake off any excess sugar, then caramelise with a blow torch until dark.

To Serve

Serve as pictured.

166
KESWICK COOKERY SCHOOL BY PETER SIDWELL

Unit 1 Sunset Hill, Keswick, Cumbria, CA12 4RN

017687 80273
www.simplygoodtaste.co.uk www.simplygoodfood.tv

Award-winning TV chef Peter Sidwell is the founder and head of Simply Good Food TV, the new iPlayer for food programming. He also owns Keswick Cookery School where he teaches and uses the facility for filming.

Simply Good Food TV now has over 300,000 viewers and that number is growing day by day. They are continuing to break boundaries with all things food and TV.

Meanwhile, back in the North West, Keswick Cookery School is located just on the edge of Keswick in the Northern Lake District. The school is surrounded by hills and stunning Lakeland scenery. It is very much a reflection of owner Peter, who has created a school that is full of culinary inspiration with herb gardens, outdoor cooking areas, a coffee bar, communal dining area and a well-equipped demo kitchen and practical kitchen for students to immerge themselves in all things food.

As a team of foodies, their main aim is to empower you with techniques and inspire you with ingredients from the local area and further afield. "We believe that after a day in the school, you will feel inspired to go home and blend our methods and approach to create your own dishes," enthuses Peter.

Keswick Cookery School also offers a private dining experience. Peter and the team create the ultimate cooking and dining experience in your home, holiday accommodation or workplace for you, your friends, family and colleagues. Always overseen by Peter, the bespoke menus are carefully designed and executed to create mouthwatering dishes using the best ingredients.

"It's like having Saturday Kitchen in your own home for the evening!"
Private dining client.

CURED LOCAL TROUT, NORDIC SEED BREAD, HORSERADISH CURD, GIN SOAKED CUCUMBER

SERVES 4

 Bedrock Gin and Tonic

Ingredients

Cured Trout

2 local trout (gutted, filleted)
4 tbsp salt
4 tbsp soft brown sugar

Gin Soaked Cucumber

½ cucumber
50ml gin

Nordic Gluten Free Seed Bread

50g flax seeds
150g mixed nuts
30g ground flax seeds
30g ground chia
5g salt
30ml oil
3 large eggs

Horseradish Curd

4 large egg yolks
2 tbsp creamed horseradish
1 lemon (juice and zest of)
250g butter (diced)
2 twists black pepper

To Serve

½ bulb fennel (thinly sliced)
8 radishes (thinly sliced)
1 handful seasonal mixed salad leaves

small loaf tin (lined with baking parchment)

Chef's Tip

This recipe is based around a few simple techniques and cracking ingredients - bring them together on a plate and enjoy! Buy the best quality ingredients you can get your hands on.

Method

For The Cured Trout (Prepare the day before)

Make 4 small cuts into the skin-side of the trout to allow the cure to permeate. Mix together the salt and sugar, then pour half of it onto a sheet of cling film. Flatten it out to ½cm thick and place the trout, skin-side down, on top. Neatly top the fillets with the remaining mix. Wrap the fish up in cling film and place in the fridge for at least 12 hours.

When the trout flesh is firm and looks like a side of smoked salmon, wash the salt mixture off well, then pat dry.

For The Gin Soaked Cucumber (Prepare the day before)

Peel the cucumber and cut it lengthways. Then, using a teaspoon, scrape out all the cucumber seeds. Using a sharp knife, cut the cucumber into small cubes and place in the gin to allow the flavours to marry together. Refrigerate overnight.

For The Nordic Gluten Free Seed Bread

Preheat the oven to 160°C (fan).

Mix all the nuts and seeds together in a bowl, then add the salt.

Mix the oil and eggs together before pouring into the bowl with the nuts and seeds. Mix well, then spoon the mixture into the prepared loaf tin and spread it out.

Bake for 20-30 minutes or until the loaf is firm. Leave the loaf to cool, then wrap in cling film until needed. Slice thinly immediately before serving.

For The Horseradish Curd

Whisk the egg yolks, horseradish, lemon juice and zest together. Place the bowl over a *bain-marie*. Add the diced butter to the egg mixture. As the bowl heats up, the butter will melt and the eggs will thicken. When thickened, remove from the heat and whisk well. Taste and check for seasoning, adding salt, pepper or lemon juice - it's up to you!

This is a simple method for making curds that have a lovely viscous texture.

To Serve

Using a sharp knife, slice the trout into long, wafer thin slices. The more surface area on the trout the better, so it's worth taking your time. We have decorated the plate this way today but when we teach this dish on our Masterchef cookery day, we very much encourage people to express themselves and decorate it with their own style; it's the taste that matters!

CUMBRIAN VENISON, PICKLED BERRIES, SMOKY TEA INFUSED POTATO

SERVES 4

 Merlot

Ingredients

Pickled Berries

100ml white wine vinegar
1 tsp honey
200g blackberries
100g blueberries

Sauce

200ml red wine
1 star anise
568ml beef stock
70g butter

Carrots

4 medium carrots
1 tsp salt

Smoky Tea Infused Potato

2 large Maris Piper potatoes (peeled)
2 Lapsang Souchong teabags
50g butter
1 tsp salt
½ tbsp ground white pepper

Venison

4 x 180g venison striploins
1 tbsp rapeseed oil
1 tsp fresh thyme (chopped)
1 tsp salt
freshly cracked black pepper

Method

For The Pickled Berries (Prepare ahead)

Place the vinegar and honey into a saucepan and bring to the boil, then add the berries and remove from the heat. Once cooled, place the berries in an airtight container and leave in the fridge until you need them. They will keep in the fridge for 8-12 weeks.

For The Sauce

Place the red wine and star anise into a pan and boil until it reduces by half. Add in the beef stock and simmer for 30 minutes until it reduces by half again. Set the sauce to one side until you are ready to cook the venison.

For The Carrots

Cook the carrots whole in salted, boiling water until *al dente*. Drain and refresh in cold water to stop the cooking process.

For The Smoky Tea Infused Potato

Cut the potatoes into quarters, place in a pan of water with the tea bags and cook until the potatoes are tender. Drain, remove the teabags and mash with plenty of butter until smooth. Season with a little salt and pepper to taste. Keep warm.

For The Venison And To Finish The Dish

Drizzle a little oil over the venison, then season with salt, pepper and thyme.

Heat a non-stick frying pan for 2-3 minutes. Add the venison to the pan and cook on all sides until the meat has a lovely rich, roasted colour. Cut the carrots lengthways and add to the pan cut-side down. When the venison is cooked to your liking, rare about 8 minutes, medium 10 minutes, remove the venison and carrots from the pan and leave to rest. Pour the red wine sauce into the hot pan and reduce a little further, then add in the butter and whisk together. Add a handful of drained pickled berries before serving.

Serve with steamed asparagus or seasonal vegetables.

Chef's Tip

Rest the venison for 3-4 minutes before serving.

CHOCOLATE & SEA SALT MARQUISE, SUMMER BERRIES, CARAMELISED OATCAKES

SERVES 4

 Prosecco! A bottle of fizz works well with this dessert.

Ingredients

Chocolate And Sea Salt Marquise

7 egg yolks
165g caster sugar
200g dark chocolate 70% (chopped)
1 tsp sea salt
250g butter (diced, softened)
65g cocoa powder
600ml double cream
1 tsp vanilla extract

Caramelised Oatcakes

100g oatcakes
100g golden caster sugar

To Serve

100ml crème fraîche
strawberry and prosecco sorbet
strawberries
raspberries
blackberries

8cm x 22cm terrine mould (greased)

Method

For The Chocolate And Sea Salt Marquise (Prepare ahead)

Line the terrine mould with cling film. Make sure that there is plenty of excess cling film over the sides of the mould.

Use an electric mixer to beat the yolks and sugar in a heatproof bowl for 5 minutes or until thick and pale. Place the bowl over a *bain-marie*. Add the chocolate and whisk for 5-6 minutes until melted. Add the salt, then drop in the butter one piece at a time, whisking between each addition until melted. Remove from the heat and fold in the cocoa powder. Allow to cool for 30 minutes.

Beat the cream and vanilla until soft peaks form. Fold a little cream into the chocolate mixture to loosen it, then fold in the remainder until combined. Pour into the prepared terrine mould, fold over the cling film to cover and refrigerate overnight.

For The Caramelised Oatcakes

Place the oatcakes into a plastic bag and, using a rolling pin, bash them up into small pieces.

Place the sugar into a large saucepan on a medium heat and cook the sugar slowly until it turns to a clear caramel. Stir in the broken oatcakes and mix well. Pour the caramelised oatcakes onto a sheet of baking parchment and leave to cool. Bash them up again into small pieces. Store in an airtight container.

To Serve

Turn the marquise out from the terrine mould and cut into slices. Serve on the caramelised oatcakes and top with the berries filled with crème fraîche. Finish the dish with a *quenelle* of strawberry and prosecco sorbet.

> **Chef's Tip**
> Cut the marquise with a warm knife for a cleaner, smoother edge.

176
THE LEATHES HEAD
COUNTRY HOUSE HOTEL & RESTAURANT

Borrowdale, Keswick, Cumbria, CA12 5UY

017687 77247
www.leatheshead.co.uk Twitter: @LeathesHead Facebook: theleatheshead

The award-winning Leathes Head is a magnificent eleven bedroom Edwardian Country House Hotel situated in the unspoilt Borrowdale Valley and just four miles south of Keswick. Recognised in 2016 as the county's 'Best Small Hotel of the Year' by Cumbria Tourism, it is set amongst three acres of private grounds and is surrounded by stunning scenery and meandering rivers. Derwentwater, the Lake District's 'Queen of the Lakes', combined with some of the most spectacular fells in the North West of England can also be easily reached directly from the hotel's doorstep.

The 2 AA Rosette restaurant, run by head chef Noel Breaks, is a true haven for food lovers. Noel is passionate about both the food and dishes he creates. Diners are treated to a menu brimming with fine dining options, impeccably prepared using locally grown and reared produce. This includes Herdwick lamb from Yew Tree Farm in Rosthwaite, local milk and free-range eggs from Scales Farm, fresh meat from Eden Valley meats and cheese from The Cheese Larder in Kendal, as well as other local Cumbrian suppliers. The dining experience is one to cherish and remember.

After your meal, it's time to retreat to the Graphite Bar and sample a local ale or choose from an ever-growing selection of craft gins.

The stylish bar has been completely refurbished using the best of Cumbrian products, skills and natural materials. The bar renovation uses Kirkstone Brathay slate, Cumbrian oak and an intricate basket light, weaved with willow harvested near Cockermouth. The interior has been crafted by local artisans for a stylish, natural and authentic feel - all overseen by design consultancy 'Other Works'.

THE LEATHES HEAD
HOTEL · RESTAURANT

With award-winning food, stylish interiors and friendly atmosphere, The Leathes Head aims to surprise and delight guests by exceeding their expectations on every occasion.

CUMBRIAN PORK BELLY, SCALLOP, CELERIAC, POPCORN

SERVES 4

 Château la Tour de l'Evêque Rosé AOC, Côtes de Provence, 2015 (France)

Ingredients

Pork Belly

365g salt
4 litres water
50g coriander seeds
1 lemon (zest of)
1 orange (zest of)
10g thyme
1 pork belly (skin on, bones removed)
vegetable oil/ duck fat (to cover)

Scallop Roe Powder And Scallops

8 scallops (roes and scallop separated)
salt (to sprinkle)
1 lime (zest of)

Pickled Celeriac

50ml water
50ml white wine vinegar
50g sugar
10 fennel seeds
10 coriander seeds
100g celeriac (cut to 1cm dice)

Celeriac Purée

100g butter
2 shallots (peeled, halved, thinly sliced)
1 celeriac (diced)
570ml chicken stock
285ml whole milk
salt and pepper

Popcorn

2 tbsp oil, salt (sprinkle of)
20g popcorn kernels
scallop roe powder

Chef's Tip

If you have access to a water bath, you can cook the pork belly *sous vide* at 82°C for 18 hours.

Method

For The Pork Belly (Allow 5 days)

Boil the salt and water together to dissolve the salt. Remove from the heat. Grind the coriander seeds, zests and thyme together and securely tie in a cloth. Place the cloth in the brine and leave to cool. Set the pork belly in a deep tray and cover with the cold brine. Refrigerate for 4 days.

Preheat the oven to 120°C.

Soak the brined belly in fresh water for 30 minutes.

Place the belly in a tray and cover with oil. Cover the tray with foil and bake for 8 hours.

Take the belly out of the oil, place between parchment paper and press, preferably overnight, in the fridge.

For The Scallop Roe Powder (Prepare ahead)

Cover the roes in salt and leave for 8 minutes. Rinse well, then dry. Place on parchment paper on a tray and sprinkle with lime zest.

Place the tray in the oven at 60°C, preferably overnight, or until the roes are dry. Blitz to a fine powder. Sieve to remove any large lumps.

For The Pickled Celeriac

Bring all the ingredients, except the celeriac, slowly to the boil, stirring. Remove from the heat, add the celeriac and leave to cool.

For The Celeriac Purée

Melt 50g of butter in a pan and *sauté* the shallots until soft. Stir in the celeriac, cook for 5 minutes. Pour in the stock and reduce to almost nothing. Add the milk, bring to the boil, then remove from the heat. Blend with the remaining butter, pass through a sieve and season.

For The Popcorn

Heat the oil and salt in a pan, stir in the kernels to coat them, then top with a lid. When they start popping, reduce the heat and shake the pan. When finished popping, remove the lid, sprinkle generously with the roe powder and stir.

To Finish And Serve

Portion the belly, cutting the skin off for a flat frying surface. Pan fry on all sides for a couple of minutes. Drain on a cloth then plate along with the purée and pickled celeriac.

Heat a pan for the scallops and lightly season them. Pan fry for 2 minutes each side, then leave to rest for 1 minute. Place next to the pork belly, add popcorn around the plate. Garnish with popcorn shoots and coriander.

YEW TREE FARM HOGGET SADDLE & BELLY, SMOKED POTATO, BABY BEETROOT, PICKLED TURNIP

SERVES 4

L'Hospitalet de Gazin, Pomerol (France)

Ingredients

Hogget Belly & Jus

½ hogget saddle (belly attached, off the bone)
2 carrots (roughly chopped)
1 onion (roughly chopped)
1 stick celery (roughly chopped)
½ bulb garlic, 2 bay leaves
2 sticks rosemary
568ml red wine
1.7 litres chicken stock
sherry vinegar (splash of)

Smoked Potato

2 Rooster potatoes (peeled)
250g butter, salt and pepper

Pickled Turnip

50ml water, 50g sugar
50ml white wine vinegar
1 sprig rosemary
1 baby turnip (finely sliced, cut into discs)

Baby Beetroot

1 bunch baby beetroot
1 tbsp red wine vinegar
285ml water

Turnip Purée

2 shallots (sliced)
50g butter
1 turnip (peeled, diced)
568ml chicken stock
285ml double cream
salt and pepper

Garnish

turnip shoots, micro coriander

smoking gun

Method

For The Hogget

Trim the saddle and belly. Trim the skin and reserve the saddle.

For The Belly (Prepare ahead)

Preheat the oven to 180°C.

Oven roast the vegetables to colour them. Roll the belly tightly and tie with string. Pan fry on all sides.

Deglaze the vegetable tray with red wine. Place a rack over the vegetables and put the belly on top. Add the stock and cover with foil. Turn the oven down to 140°C and cook the belly for 3 hours. Roll tightly in cling film and leave to cool.

For The Hogget Jus

Pass the stock from the belly pan through a sieve. Leave to cool. Remove all the fat from the top of the container. Place the stock in a pan and reduce. Finish with a touch of sherry vinegar.

For The Smoked Potato

Using an apple corer, punch out rounds of potato and place in water for 30 minutes.

Put the block of butter in an airtight container and fill with smoke using a smoking gun. Place the lid on, leave to infuse for 3 minutes and repeat 3 times. Repeat for the potatoes.

Melt the butter in a pan, add the potatoes and seasoning. Cook slowly, turning the potatoes, until tender.

For The Pickled Turnip

Gently bring all the ingredients, except the turnip, to the boil stirring occasionally. Add the turnip and leave to cool.

For The Baby Beetroot

Bring everything to the boil, then simmer for 15 minutes. Cool. Rub the skins off the beets and return to the stock.

For The Turnip Purée

Cook the shallots in the butter until tender. Add the turnip and cook out a little. Pour in the stock and reduce until almost evaporated. Add the double cream and bring to the boil. Blitz in a blender. Pass through a sieve, then season.

To Serve

Preheat the oven to 180°C.

Cut the hogget saddle into 4 pieces and season. Pan fry skin-side down until golden, turn over and seal. Place skin-side down again and cook in the oven for 8 minutes, then rest for 8 minutes, turning halfway through resting. Serve as pictured.

GARDEN RHUBARB, TONKA BEAN MOUSSE, HONEYCOMB, THYME ICE CREAM

SERVES 6

 Château Septy (France)

Ingredients

Thyme Ice Cream

1 litre whole milk
20g thyme
180g egg yolk
200g caster sugar
70g milk powder
50ml whipping cream

Honeycomb

200g caster sugar
70g glucose
40g clear honey
5 tbsp water
10g bicarbonate of soda

Tonka Bean Mousse

300ml double cream
½ tonka bean (grated)
100g caster sugar
3 egg yolks
3 leaves gelatine (softened in cold water)
150ml double cream (lightly whipped)

Poached Rhubarb And Crisps

500g sugar
500ml water
2 tbsp grenadine
4 sticks rhubarb (cut into 5cm batons)

Chef's Tip

If you don't have access to tonka bean, vanilla will substitute nicely.

Method

For The Thyme Ice Cream (Prepare ahead)
Bring the milk to the boil, add the thyme, take off the heat and leave to infuse for 1 hour.
Whisk the egg yolk and sugar together until pale. Add the milk powder and cream into the milk and bring back to the boil. Pour over the egg yolk mix and whisk until well incorporated.
Place the mix back into a pan and, on a medium heat while continuously stirring, bring to 82°C. Pass the mix through a sieve into a container and cool over ice water. Refrigerate for 24 hours to mature the flavour, then churn in an ice cream machine.

For The Honeycomb
Line a tray with parchment paper. Place all the ingredients, except the bicarbonate of soda, in a deep pan and bring to a light caramel. Whisk in the bicarbonate of soda, then pour onto the tray. Score with a knife while hot. When cool, break up and store in an airtight tub.
Preheat the oven to 150°C.
Blitz a handful of honeycomb to a fine powder. Sieve the powder onto a tray lined with parchment. Bake for 2 minutes. When dissolved to a glass-like effect, leave to cool. Break into shards and store in an airtight tub.

For The Tonka Bean Mousse
Bring the cream and tonka bean to the boil, remove from the heat and leave to infuse for 30 minutes.
Mix the sugar and egg yolks together.
Warm the tonka cream, then pour over the egg mix. Return the mix to a pan and cook out over a medium heat to 82°C.
Stir in the gelatine and pass through a sieve into a mixing bowl, reserve to one side.
Once the mix has started to set, fold in the whipped cream and place in the fridge to set. Once set, beat until smooth and place in a piping bag. Reserve in the fridge.

For The Poached Rhubarb And Crisps
Warm the sugar, water and grenadine, stirring occasionally until the sugar has dissolved. Bring the syrup to 70°C. Place three quarters of the batons in the syrup for 10 minutes. Remove from the syrup, place on a tray and leave to cool. Reserve for later.
Thinly slice the remaining batons, dip them into the cool syrup and dry on an all-purpose cloth to soak up any excess syrup. Lay the rhubarb slices on a cling film lined tray and place in the oven (60°C) for 40 minutes or until completely dry.

To Serve
Serve as pictured.

186
LUNYA

18-20 College Lane, Liverpool One, Liverpool, L1 3DS
Barton Arcade, Deansgate, Manchester, M3 2BB

Liverpool: 0151 706 9770. Manchester: 0161 413 3317
www.lunya.co.uk Twitter: @lunya @lunyamcr Facebook: Lunya

Lunya is the award-winning Catalonian deli, restaurant and bar set up by Peter and Elaine Kinsella in Liverpool in 2010 and now in Manchester, with plans for further modest growth. Based on an ongoing love affair with Catalan and Spanish gastronomy and their eating out culture, Peter and Elaine have recreated the taste of the best, modern tapas bars in Barcelona here in the North West. With great critical acclaim from the national press (The Guardian, Sunday Times and Telegraph have all included it in their 'best of/top 50' lists of UK restaurants) they are also the winners (for an unprecedented two times) of the Good Food Guide North West Restaurant of the Year and both Liverpool Restaurant of the Year and Manchester Restaurant of the Year.

Lunya's deli is a temple to the very best food to come from Spain with over 40 artisan cheeses, Serrano and Ibérico hams carved off the bone and over 1300 other food and drink products to satisfy the most demanding foodie, including chorizo and other cured meats, a huge selection of anchovies and other seafood, as well as chocolates and confectionary galore.

The restaurant serves both traditional and modern tapas, paella, suckling pig and huge deli platters. Obsessive about the very best quality ingredients and always determined to make everything themselves, Lunya's team of talented chefs produce some of the very best Spanish food in the UK. A place for shoppers, business diners, families and friends celebrating and great for celebrity spotting, it is no wonder that El Mundo named Lunya in their list of the 10 best things to do in the UK for any Spanish tourist visiting the UK.

With an online store delivering across the UK and beyond, it really is your place for anything Spanish.

Location photographs by Howard Rollinson and Natalia Castillejo

Passion on a plate, Lunya uses the very best freshest ingredients and creates tapas of pure perfection.

FRITO MARISCO

SERVES 4

🍷 *Avancia Godello, D.O. Monterrei
(Spain)*

Ingredients

Frito Marisco

1 medium waxy potato (peeled, cut into 1 cm dice)
25ml olive oil
1 clove garlic (crushed)
1 bay leaf
½ red pepper (deseeded, cut into 1cm dice)
2 spring onions (cut into ½ cm discs)
200g calamari (cut into 1cm pieces)
100g peeled raw prawns
16 mussels (meat of)
20g fresh garden peas
2g fennel seeds
1 tsp pimentón dulce
salt (to taste)

Method

For The Frito Marisco

Add the diced potato to a pan of boiling water and cook until just turning soft, remove and drain. Set aside for later.

Heat the olive oil in a large frying pan and add the crushed garlic and bay leaf. After 1 minute add the red peppers and fry over a medium heat for another minute. Add the spring onions, fry for another minute then, with a slotted spoon, remove all the vegetables and set aside with the potatoes.

Add the calamari to the frying pan and fry until the calamari just starts to change colour, then add the prawns and mussel meat. Fry for 2 minutes until the prawns have changed colour and are cooked.

Now add in the cooked vegetables, peas, fennel seed, pimentón and salt and mix well in the pan. It is ready to eat immediately.

Chef's Tip

Inspired by the seafood dishes of Majorca, you can use any combination of seafood for this delightful dish.

POLLO AL MORO

SERVES 4

🍷 *Abadal 3.9, Shiraz/Cabernet Sauvignon, DO Pla de Bages (Spain)*

Ingredients

Pollo Al Moro

1kg boneless chicken thighs
50ml olive oil
1½ onions (quartered)
1 red chilli (roughly chopped)
½ lemon (juice of)
4 stalks fresh coriander (roughly chopped)
1 tsp ground cumin
1 tsp dried oregano
1 clove garlic (finely chopped)
10 saffron threads
1 dstp Ras al Hanout
¾ litres chicken stock
salt and pepper to taste

To Serve

pomegranate seeds
pomegranate molasses (drizzle of)
fresh coriander

Method

For The Pollo Al Moro

Brown the chicken over a high heat with the olive oil in a frying pan. Remove the chicken with a slotted spoon, leaving the oil behind.

Blitz all the vegetables, garlic, herbs and spices to a paste in a food processor. You may need to add 50ml of water to aid this.

Fry the paste gently in the frying pan in the oil for 5 minutes over a medium heat. Add the chicken and fry for another 5 minutes.

Pour in the chicken stock and bring to a simmer. Simmer gently over a low heat for 1 hour.

If the sauce has not reduced enough (you want it thick enough to coat the chicken), remove the chicken and bring the sauce to the boil until it has reduced further. Add the chicken back to the pan.

To Serve

Serve garnished with pomegranate seeds, a drizzle of pomegranate molasses and fresh coriander.

Chef's Tip

Originating from Girona in Catalunya, this recipe is an adaptation of a dish from centuries ago when the Moors invaded Catalunya. Serve it with chickpeas for a delightful combination.

BURNT SAN SEBASTIAN CHEESECAKE

SERVES 6

🍷 *Victoria Moscatel, DO Malaga*
(Spain)

Ingredients

Cheesecake

500g cream cheese
250ml double cream
3 large eggs
175g caster sugar
½ tsp vanilla essence
½ tbsp plain flour

To Serve

roasted hazelnuts
raisins (soaked in PX sherry)

18cm clip-on cake tin (greased with softened butter, lined)

Method

For The Cheesecake

Preheat the oven to 220°C (fan).

Beat all the ingredients together in a large bowl with a whisk until a smooth batter is achieved.

Pour into the prepared cake tin and bake for 50-60 minutes.

To test if the cheesecake is ready, pierce the centre with a small knife, the knife should come out clean. The top and sides should have some 'burnt' parts, being dark brown in places.

Allow the cheesecake to cool, take out of the tin and refrigerate.

To Serve

Serve as pictured garnished with roasted hazelnuts and raisins soaked in PX sherry.

> **Chef's Tip**
> A very hot oven and bravery is needed to create the classic burnt crust, made famous by La Viña of San Sebastian.

196 MANCHESTER HOUSE

18-22 Bridge Street, Spinningfields, Manchester, M3 3BZ

0161 835 2557
www.manchesterhouse.uk.com Twitter: @MCRHouse Facebook: Manchester House

n just four years, Manchester House has firmly established itself as one of the premier dining venues in the North West.

The creation of acclaimed chef Aiden Byrne and the late restaurateur Tim Bacon, it has earned 4 AA Rosettes and a host of other accolades. Byrne and Bacon decided to form the restaurant through a shared passion for fine dining and a desire to 'feed Manchester'. Their collaboration has been a remarkable success and the desirable second floor restaurant has earned a stellar reputation.

The restaurant was informed by its location, so a thoroughly modern interior hints at Manchester's industrial past with wood, concrete and cotton all present in a spacious dining room. The food is sublime with the freshest, seasonal ingredients offered in alluring, technical dishes.

Byrne was raised in Merseyside and comes from a humble background. Head chef by the tender age of 22 and a Michelin star winner, he has worked in many Michelin starred establishments including Adlards, Tom Aikens, Pied A Terre and The Commons.

Aiden spent a long time in London mastering his skills and focusing his passion. Yearning to move closer to home with his family, Aiden opened Manchester House with Tim Bacon's Living Ventures in 2013.

It was a passion project which has won Aiden both critical acclaim and a loyal fan base.

Tasting menus are served daily. Expect to start with puffed pork crackling with smoked apple and hazelnut, followed by crisp chicken skin with foie gras mousse and aged Parmesan before a roasted langoustine with ajwain, smoked cauliflower and venison carpaccio, then a braised beef cheek with Txogitxu tartare and choucroute. For dessert, Manchester tart ice cream, finishing with goat's curd with tarragon, pine nuts and blackberry.

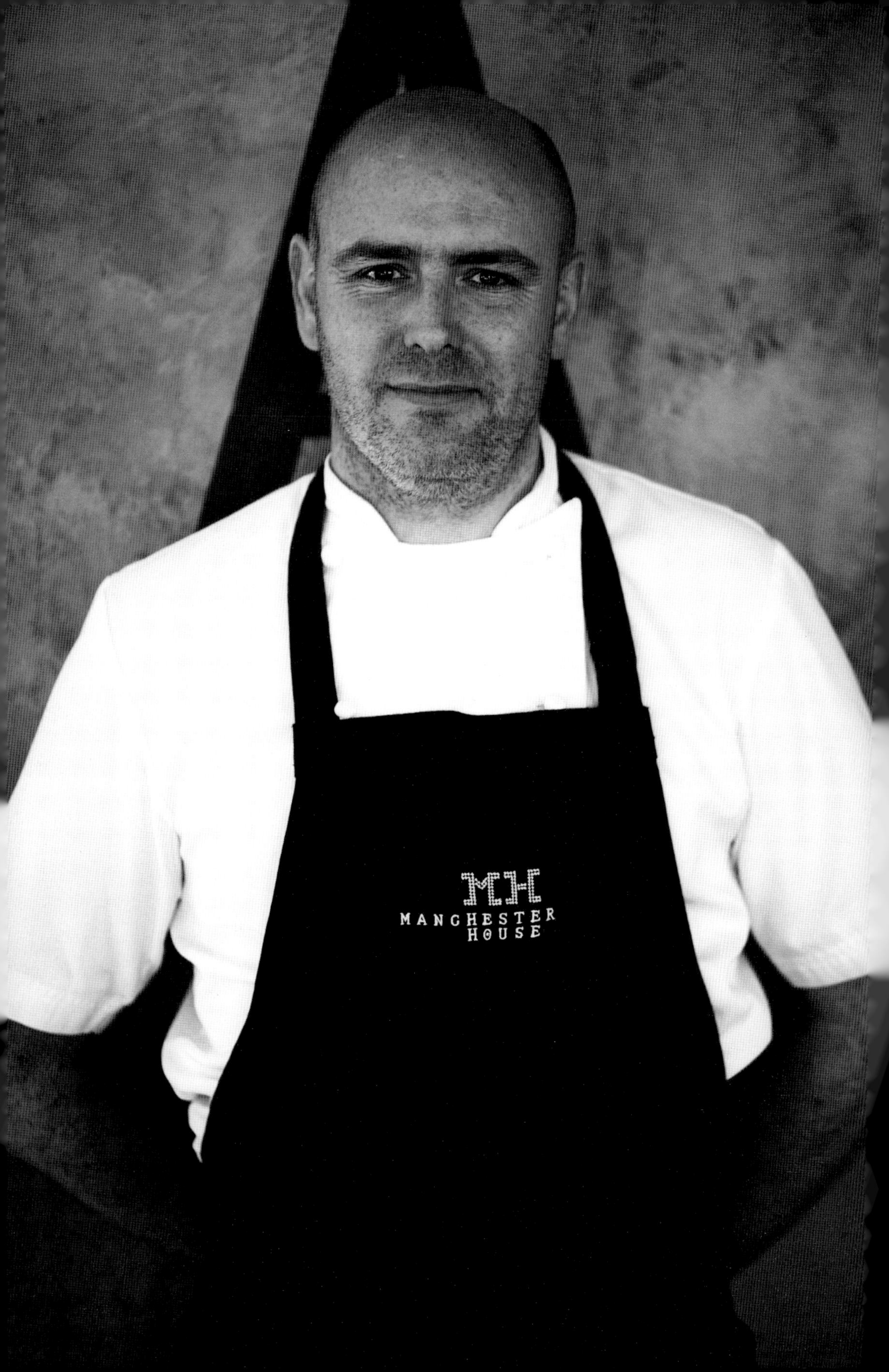
MH
MANCHESTER
HOUSE

Manchester House is home to chef patron Aiden Byrne and his loyal serving team. Aiden's career is steeped in traditionalism and his flavour combinations stay true to classical marriages.

CRISP CHICKEN SKIN, SMOKED FOIE GRAS MOUSSE, AGED REGGIANO, PICKLED ONIONS

SERVES 6

Long Beach Chenin Blanc, 2015, Robertson
(South Africa)

Ingredients

Pickled Onions

200g silverskin onions (peeled)
100ml water
100ml distilled malt vinegar
20g caster sugar
2g pink peppercorns
2 bay leaves, 2g thyme, 2g garlic

White Onion And Parmesan Purée

500g Italian white onions (sliced)
250ml double cream
16g Parmesan powder
25g unsalted butter
Maldon sea salt (to taste)

Smoked Foie Gras Mousse

100g oak smoking chips
100ml water
300g foie gras (frozen, sliced)
125g eggs (about 2½ eggs)
200ml double cream
3.6g pink salt
Maldon sea salt (to taste)

Smoked Foie Gras, White Onion And Parmesan Mousse

500g white onion and Parmesan purée
500g smoked foie gras mousse
14g bronze gelatine leaf (softened in cold water)

Crisp Chicken Skin

6 large pieces chicken skin
Maldon sea salt (to season)

To Serve

36 month aged Parmesan (finely grated)

Method

For The Pickled Onions

Slice the silverskin onions on a mandoline to 2mm. Place the remaining ingredients into a heavy-based pan and bring to the boil. Remove from the heat and add the onions. Decant into an airtight jar and place in the fridge for at least 5 hours.

For The White Onion And Parmesan Purée

Add the onions and cream to a pan and cover. Bring to the boil, then simmer for 6 minutes. Blend for 4 minutes. Season with Parmesan powder and salt. Slightly overseason as this will be eaten cold.

For The Smoked Foie Gras Mousse

Vacuum pack the oak chips and water at full strength. Set aside for 1 hour.

Line a deep half gastro tray with tin foil. Put the damp smoking chips on the foil and place on the stove. When it starts smoking, lay a perforated tray over the top with the frozen foie gras slices evenly spaced inside. Tightly cover the trays with 2 layers of foil and gently smoke for 10 minutes until a light golden colour.

Gently warm the smoked foie gras, eggs and cream to 37°C. Blend until smooth, then season with pink salt - the mix should taste slightly overseasoned. Season with Maldon, if required. Pass through a fine *chinois* into a deep, metal tray. Cling film and steam at 85°C for 10 minutes. The mousse should firm up but retain a slight wobble. Set aside to cool, but not to go cold.

> **Chef's Tip**
> It is important that the foie gras is frozen so it smokes and does not cook.

For The Smoked Foie Gras, White Onion And Parmesan Mousse

Warm the onion purée to 40°C and stir in the gelatine. Gently fold the purée into the warm foie gras mousse, transfer to a piping bag with a 9mm round piping nozzle and set in the fridge.

For The Crisp Chicken Skin

Preheat the oven to 160°C.

Line a heavy, flat tray with greaseproof paper and stretch the chicken skin out on it. Season generously with salt. Cover with a layer of greaseproof paper and a heavy, flat tray. Roast for 30 minutes. Cool on a wire rack.

To Serve

Plate as pictured.

TURBOT CARPACCIO, GRILLED ASPARAGUS, PINE SPRUCE, RHUBARB, LEMON CONFIT

SERVES 6

 Baron de Badassiere Viognier, 2015
(Languedoc, France)

Ingredients

Confit Lemons

10 unwaxed lemons (2cm deep cross cut in 1 end)
water (as required)
fine sea salt (30g per litre of water)

Turbot

1 x 4-5kg turbot
Maldon sea salt (as required)

Pickled Rhubarb

3 large stems forced Yorkshire rhubarb (cut into
10cm batons)
500ml water
500ml Champagne vinegar
100g caster sugar
10g pink peppercorns

Lemon Confit Purée

10 *confit* lemons
100g caster sugar (plus extra for seasoning)
1 litre water
lemon juice (to taste)

Pine Spruce Oil

200ml cold pressed rapeseed oil (warmed to 55°C)
100g pine spruce tips

Wye Valley Asparagus

14 spears Wye Valley jumbo asparagus (trimmed
and woody stems removed)
olive oil (as required)
Maldon sea salt (to taste)

Garnish

3 young breakfast radishes (halved)
pine spruce tips and buds
Maldon sea salt
freshly milled black pepper
olive oil

large airtight glass container (sterilised)

Method

For The Confit Lemons (Prepare 10 days in advance)

Boil the lemons in water for 3 minutes. Strain. Repeat 3 times.

Place a large pan, with slightly more water than you will need to fill the jar, on the stove and season heavily with salt. Boil the lemons for 5 minutes, then transfer to the jar and top up with hot water. Cool to 45°C. Secure and store in a cool, dark place for 10 days.

For The Turbot

Lay the turbot skirts (fins), not touching, in a vac pack bag in a single layer. Season. Seal at 100% on 'soft vac' and steam for 10 minutes. When still warm, pop out the skirts and refrigerate.

Cut the centre piece from the largest fillet, around 12cm long. Wrap in cling film and freeze. When frozen, slice on a meat slicer 3mm thick. Refrigerate between greaseproof paper. You will need 6 slices.

For The Pickled Rhubarb

Slice the batons lengthways 2mm thick on a mandoline. Add the remaining ingredients to a pan and bring to the boil. Remove from the heat and cool slightly. Add the rhubarb, then transfer to a Kilner jar, leave to cool.

For The Lemon Confit Purée

Drain the *confit* lemons and place in cold water for 10 minutes. Dice the flesh into 1cm pieces, then add to a pan with the sugar and cover with water. Reduce until the water has almost all gone. Blend for 4 minutes. Push through a fine *chinois* and season with lemon juice and caster sugar. Refrigerate in a squeezy bottle.

For The Pine Spruce Oil

Blend the ingredients for 4 minutes, then leave to infuse for 2 hours. Pass through a muslin lined sieve and discard any solids. Store in an airtight jar.

For The Wye Valley Asparagus

Slice 8 spears lengthways on a mandoline 2mm thick. Dress the best 24 central slices with a little olive oil and salt.

Blanch the tips of the remaining asparagus for 10 seconds, then chill in iced water. Pat dry. Cut in half lengthways, then refrigerate.

To Serve

Scorch the asparagus slices for 10 seconds on a griddle. Transfer to a plate. Curl the rhubarb ribbons onto the centre of the asparagus. Layer over the turbot carpaccio and season with salt. Dot with lemon purée. Place the turbot skirt into a bowl with the asparagus tips and dress with olive oil, salt and pepper, then add to the plate. Drizzle with pine spruce oil and garnish as pictured.

MANCHESTER TART ICE CREAM

SERVES 6

🍷 *Innocent Bystander Moscato Rose, 2014*
(Victoria, Australia)

Ingredients

Coconut Ice Cream

530g coconut purée
100ml double cream
95g egg yolks
120g caster sugar

Raspberry Sorbet

200g coconut purée
70g caster sugar
20g glucose
300g raspberry purée

Crumble

50g plain flour
50g unsalted butter
50g icing sugar
50g ground almonds

Lavender Meringues

22g caster sugar
115g egg whites
purple food colouring (blue and red)

Raspberry Wafers

37g egg whites
2½g xanthan gum
200g raspberry purée

Garnish

desiccated coconut

Method

For The Coconut Ice Cream

Heat the coconut purée with the cream. Whisk the yolks and sugar together.

When the cream reaches the boil, pour it onto the yolks and mix. Return it to the pan and cook out, stirring continuously until it reaches 63°C. Cool in a bowl set over ice. Fill a Paco beaker and freeze. Alternatively, churn in an ice cream machine.

For The Raspberry Sorbet

Warm the coconut purée and dissolve the sugar and glucose in it. Remove from the heat and add the raspberry purée. Freeze in a Paco beaker. Alternatively, churn in an ice cream machine.

For The Crumble

Preheat the oven to 170°C.

Place all the ingredients into a food processor with a paddle and mix to a crumb. Spread on a tray and bake until just golden, about 10-12 minutes. Chop with a knife, whilst hot, to small, even-sized crumbs.

For The Lavender Meringues (Prepare in advance)

Preheat the oven to 50°C.

Place the sugar and egg whites in a mixer bowl over a *bain-marie*. Warm the mix to 38°C, whisking or stirring frequently to dissolve the sugar. When at temperature, attach the bowl to the mixer, then whisk on high speed until cool, adding the colouring whilst whisking. Spread the mix thinly onto silicone mats and dehydrate for 12 hours. Store in an airtight container.

For The Raspberry Wafers (Prepare in advance)

Preheat the oven to 50°C.

Blend the egg whites and xanthan gum in a blender until really thick. Add the raspberry purée. Transfer to a mixer with a whisk attachment, whisk for 5-7 minutes. The mix will increase in size and be paler in colour. Spread, ½cm thick, onto silicone mats and dehydrate for 12 hours. Store in an airtight container.

To Serve

Quenelle the ice cream and sorbet. Crush the wafers, meringues and combine with the chopped crumble. Roll the ice cream and sorbet in the crumble mix, if desired, then sprinkle with desiccated coconut. Serve as pictured.

> **Chef's Tip**
> You can prepare all elements of this dish in advance.

206
NUTTERS
RESTAURANT

Edenfield Road, Norden, Rochdale, OL12 7TT

01706 650 167
www.nuttersrestaurant.co.uk Twitter: @nuttersofficial Facebook: Nutters Restaurant Official

Not just a meal, but an adventure.

Nutters Restaurant is the playground of celebrity chef Andrew Nutter. Set in six and a half acres of beautifully restored parkland, this 18th Century manor house elegantly combines the new with old and boasts spectacular views across Ashworth Valley and Greater Manchester.

The business which started in 1993 has seen it grow from a 40 seater restaurant at the New Inn Pub near Owd Betts to the magical site where it is now. The main restaurant seats 150 diners with additional dining in the private rooms accommodating up to 120 guests, providing the perfect venue for civil wedding ceremonies, cocktail parties and lavish receptions.

Andrew truly has a unique setting to showcase the very best of local and regional produce - something he is a passionate advocate of. Working closely with local suppliers, he is able to source the finest ingredients. Local fish from the Flyde Coast, turbot, brill, megrin are key examples, as is the venison from the Tatton Estate, Limousin beef from the North West or the great crop of local vegetables from the region.

Whether it be a light lunch, romantic dinner or sumptuous afternoon tea, a Nutter meal is always an experience of interesting flavours and unusual combinations but, above all, it's a meal to be enjoyed in beautiful surroundings, safe in the confidence of the quality of the ingredients and the attentiveness of the staff.

Using only the very best local and regional produce, let Andrew and his team take you on a culinary adventure and introduce you to 'The Art of Seriously Good Cooking'.

ROAST SEA BASS, WHITE & GREEN ENGLISH ASPARAGUS, CHIVE EMULSION

SERVES 4

 Riesling, Turckheim Vieilles Vignes (France)

Ingredients

Vegetables

1 bunch white asparagus
1 tbsp olive oil
salt and pepper
1 bunch green English asparagus
1 small Romanesco (cut into florets)

Chive Emulsion

2 egg yolks
2 tsp Dijon mustard
1 tbsp white wine vinegar
1 tbsp chopped chives
200ml olive oil
salt and pepper

Wild Garlic Oil

1 handful wild garlic
4 tbsp olive oil

Roast Sea Bass

1 tbsp olive oil
4 x 160g sea bass fillets
1 clove garlic (finely chopped)
1 lemon (juice and zest of)

Garnish

garlic and other edible flowers

Method

For The Vegetables

Cut the white asparagus in half, then roll in the olive oil. Char on a griddle pan and season well. *Blanch* the green asparagus and Romanesco until *al dente*.

For The Chive Emulsion

Place the egg yolks, Dijon mustard and vinegar into a deep measuring jug and blend with a hand blender. Add the chives and pour in the oil, blending as you do so to create an *emulsified* cream. Season to taste.

For The Wild Garlic Oil

Simply blend the wild garlic and oil together.

For The Roast Sea Bass

When ready to serve, heat a non-stick pan, add a splash of olive and sear the sea bass skin-side down until lightly coloured. Turn over, then add the garlic and lemon zest to the pan basting the fish in the now lemon and garlic oil.

To Serve

Arrange the griddled and *blanched* vegetables on plates. Drizzle with the chive *emulsion* and garlic oil. Season well. Place the fish on top and finish with a squeeze of lemon juice and a flourish of edible flowers.

Chef's Tip

All the dressings can be made beforehand and kept in the refrigerator so no last minute panicking. Simplicity is the key - let the produce take centre stage.

HAREFIELD PREMIER BEEF FILLET, CELERIAC PUREE, EMMALIE POTATOES, FRAZZLED PANCETTA

SERVES 4

 Juan Gil Blue Label 18 Meses Monastrell
(Jumilla, Spain)

Ingredients

Beef Fillet

1 clove garlic (finely chopped)
fresh thyme and rosemary (few sprigs, chopped)
700g barrel fillet
salt and pepper
1 tbsp olive oil
butter (knob of)

Celeriac Purée

½ celeriac (trimmed)
200ml double cream
125g butter
salt and pepper

Mushroom And Spinach Fricassée

1 tbsp olive oil
1 shallot (finely chopped)
1 clove garlic (finely chopped)
100g mixed wild mushrooms
2 handfuls leaf spinach

Potatoes

12 Emmalie new potatoes (*blanched*)
1 tbsp olive oil
2 tbsp diced pancetta

Method

For The Beef Fillet (Prepare ahead)

Mix together the garlic, thyme and rosemary and roll the beef fillet in it. Roll in cling film tightly and leave the fillet for at least 2 hours.

> **Chef's Tip**
> If possible, leave the meat to marinate in the herbs overnight.

For The Celeriac Purée

Dice the celeriac into 2cm cubes. Place in a pan with the cream and butter and cover with a lid. Cook on a low heat for approximately 20 minutes until soft. Blend until smooth and season.

For The Mushroom And Spinach Fricassée

Gently heat the olive oil in a small frying pan, then fry the shallot and garlic together until softened. Add the wild mushrooms and cook for a couple of minutes, then add the spinach to wilt.

For The Potatoes

Preheat the oven to 180°C.

Using a knife, *turn* the potatoes into barrels to reveal the pink flesh. Place on a tray with the olive oil and the pancetta and roast in the oven for 5 minutes.

To Cook The Beef Fillet

Preheat the oven to 180°C.

Remove the cling film from the beef and season well. Heat the olive oil in a frying pan and add the butter. When hot, seal the fillet until a deep golden. Roast in the oven for 16 minutes. Remove from the oven and leave to rest.

To Serve

Place a spoonful of celeriac purée in the middle of each plate. Spoon around the mushroom and spinach fricassée and the potatoes. Slice the fillet into 4 and place a quarter on each plate.

MANGO DELICE, ALFONSO MANGO SORBET

SERVES 8

 Elysium Black Muscat (USA)

Ingredients

Base
200g Hob Nob biscuits
60g butter (melted)

Filling
3 leaves gelatine
80g mango purée
250g cream cheese
80g caster sugar
250g whipping cream (semi-whipped)

Topping
1 leaf gelatine
100g mango purée
100g caster sugar
100ml water

Alfonso Mango Sorbet
250g sugar
250ml water
½ vanilla pod
450g Alfonso mango purée
2 lemons (juice of)

To Finish
Alfonso mango slices
raspberries
biscuit crumb
edible flowers
mango sugar tuile (optional)

15cm x 30cm tray (lined with cling film)

Method

For The Base
Blitz the Hob Nobs to a light crumb, then add the butter. Use a metal spoon to press the biscuit crumbs down firmly and evenly into the base of the prepared tray. Place in the fridge to firm.

For The Filling
Soak the gelatine in the mango purée for 20 minutes, then warm gently until melted. Cream together the cream cheese and sugar until light, mix in the mango purée, then fold in the semi-whipped cream.

Spoon this mixture on top of the biscuit base and level with a palette knife. Place in the fridge to firm up, about 4 hours.

For The Topping
Soak the gelatine in the mango purée, sugar and water for 20 minutes, then warm gently to melt. Cool slightly, then pour over the top of the delice.

Place in the fridge for 2 hours to firm. Remove from the tray with the assistance of pulling on the cling film.

For The Alfonso Mango Sorbet (Makes approximately 1 litre)
Make a stock syrup by gently heating the sugar in the water with the vanilla pod until dissolved. Bring to the boil, remove from the heat and leave to infuse until cool.

Place 375ml of the cool stock syrup in a food processor, add the mango purée and lemon juice and blend. Pass through a sieve. Churn in an ice cream machine until smooth and firm. Serve straight away or place in the freezer. Try to eat within a few days otherwise it will lose its smooth consistency and will have formed ice crystals.

To Serve
Slice into 8 rectangles and plate. Sit a *quenelle* of the mango sorbet on a little biscuit crumb, then finish with mango slices, raspberries, mango sugar tuile and edible flowers.

> **Chef's Tip**
> A great elegant dinner party recipe that oozes extravagance. Do try and source the Alfonso mango; when in season, the sweet honey flavour is seriously hard to beat.

216
THE PUNCH BOWL INN

Crosthwaite, Lyth Valley, Cumbria, LA8 8HR

015395 68237
www.the-punchbowl.co.uk Twitter: @PunchBowlInn Facebook: The Punch Bowl Inn at Crosthwaite

The Punch Bowl Inn and Restaurant at Crosthwaite is tucked away in the heart of the unspoilt Lyth Valley countryside, next door to the Parish Church of St Mary's. The history as an inn dates back as far as 1829 when it was also used as a blacksmiths.

Today, The Punch Bowl has been extensively refurbished and offers a relaxing blend of old English pub charm with new, modern comforts. The friendly atmosphere stretches through its lounge, bar and stylish restaurant. Nine gorgeous bedrooms are full of character and homely charm and the luxurious bathrooms all have underfloor heating, roll top baths and monsoon showers. The stunning valley views from some of the rooms capture the heart of the area including its abundance of damsons and damson blossom in the springtime.

An inn for all seasons. The Punch Bowl's outdoor terrace is a perfect place to enjoy alfresco dining in the sunshine and, in colder months, the snug dining areas with sumptuous leather sofas and crackling log fires are ever-popular places for guests to relax and enjoy fine, flavoursome food, local real ales and a pretty impressive wine list. The friendly, attentive staff are used to guests returning time and time again to experience some of the best of the Lake District's hospitality in stunning surroundings.

The Punch Bowl's award-winning 2 AA Rosette menus, created by head chef Arthur Bridgeman Quin and his team, are served all week in both the contemporary restaurant and beamed lounge dining area with cosy log burner. Arthur is now in his fifth year at The Punch Bowl, having joined straight from school and whilst continuing his catering studies at Kendal College. In 2016, he was awarded the title of 'UK Young Chef of the Year' at the Craft Guild of Chef's Awards - the annual chefs' Oscars. Despite his success, Arthur's feet are firmly on the ground and he's definitely not one for a lot of fuss. In his words, "the work is reward enough" as he is doing the job he loves with a team that are constantly teaching and challenging each other. They are fully dedicated and are always pushing themselves to continually raise the standards for The Punch Bowl customers. Menus are exciting and creative and push the boundaries of traditional pub food; they are passionate about working with local producers to showcase the best of the area and always use the best quality, locally sourced, seasonal produce.

THE
PUNCH
BOWL
INN &
RESTAURANT

RECEPTION

The Punch Bowl's aim for all guests is to create a home away from home where they can relax, unwind and be well and truly spoiled.

SEARED SCALLOPS, CARROT, CHICKEN WINGS

SERVES 4

 *Viognier, Casa de Lolol (Chile)*

Ingredients

Chicken Wings
8 chicken wings
250g duck fat

Chicken Jus
150g chicken wings
1 shallot (chopped)
1 clove garlic
1 sprig fresh thyme
1 litre chicken stock
125ml white wine

Carrot Pickle
8 baby carrots
300ml white wine vinegar
200ml water
100g sugar

Carrot Purée
1kg baby carrots (leafy tops reserved)
100g butter
400ml double cream
2 cardamom pods
salt (pinch of)

Scallops
12 king scallops (we use Loch Fyne)
½ lemon (spritz of)
25g butter
3 tbsp rapeseed oil

Garnish
8 baby carrots

Method

For The Chicken Wings

Preheat the oven to 120°C (fan).

Confit the wings by covering them in the duck fat and cooking slowly in the oven for 2 hours. When cooked, push the bone out and discard. Set the wings aside, ready to sear in the pan with the scallops.

For The Chicken Jus

Preheat the oven to 180°C (fan).

Roast the chicken wings in an ovenproof pan until golden, about 20 minutes.

Remove from the oven and place onto the stove top. Add the shallot to the pan with the garlic and thyme, then *deglaze* the pan with the wine and stock. Reduce until silky. When the jus lightly covers the back of a spoon, pass through a *chinois*.

For The Carrot Pickle

Slice the carrots into very thin ribbons. Add to a pan with the white wine vinegar, water and sugar. Bring to the boil, then remove from the heat and leave to cool for 1 hour.

For The Carrot Purée

Add all the ingredients to a pan and, over a low to medium heat, cook slowly for about 30 minutes.

Remove the cardamom pods. Purée the mixture and pass through a fine sieve. Keep warm.

For The Scallops

Open the shells carefully and remove the roe, wash quickly in very cold water (3 seconds). Cook the scallops in 2 batches. Heat half the butter and oil in a frying pan. Add half the *confit* chicken wings to the pan and heat, add 6 scallops to the pan, sear them, then turn over and cook for 1 minute. Spritz with lemon juice. Repeat for the remaining wings and scallops.

Chef's Tip

Try and use fresh scallops, not frozen. Quick fire frying them keeps them succulent and sweet.

For The Garnish

Wash and pat dry the carrot top leaves. Poach the baby carrots in boiling, salted water for 3-4 minutes.

To Serve

Arrange the baby carrots on top of the scallops and serve as pictured with the pickled carrot ribbons.

ROAST GOOSNARGH DUCK, BEETROOT, ORANGE, DUCK FAT CHIPS

SERVES 4

 Pinot Noir, Gran Reserva
(Chile)

Ingredients

Roast Duck

1 x 1.4kg duck
500g duck fat, 50g soft butter

Beetroot

50g smoked bacon or pancetta (diced)
4 fresh beetroot (grated)
1 shallot (sliced)
1 clove garlic (chopped)
1 sprig fresh thyme
75ml ruby port
25ml red wine vinegar
salt and pepper

Duck Fat Chips

6 Maris Piper potatoes (peeled, cut into cylinders)
500g duck fat, 500ml rapeseed oil

Damson Purée

600g damsons (stones removed)
200ml water
200g sugar
salt (pinch of)

Duck Jus

1 duck carcass
1 shallot (chopped)
1 clove garlic
1 sprig fresh thyme
125ml white wine
1 litre chicken stock
1 orange (segments of)

Thyme Oil

100g thyme
100ml rapeseed oil

Kale

300g kale (weight with stalks), 10g butter
oil (to deep fry)

Method

For The Roast Duck

Preheat the oven to 120°C (fan).
Remove the legs and place in the duck fat. *Confit* in the oven for 3 hours. Remove the bones and lay the legs onto a baking tray. Press a weighted tray on top.
Preheat the oven to 190°C (fan).
Lightly score the breast fat on the duck crown. Rub with butter, then roast for 12-14 minutes. Rest for the same length of time. Remove the breasts and slice thinly, allowing 3 slices per person.

For The Beetroot

Pan fry the bacon, then add all the ingredients and cook until tender, about 25 minutes. Season to taste.

For The Duck Fat Chips

Combine the oil and fat and heat to 130°C. Cook the potatoes for 12 minutes, then remove. Heat the oil and fat to 180°C. Return the chips to the oil and cook until golden brown.

> **Chef's Tip**
> The chips can be made in advance and finished off with a second fry when ready to serve.

For The Damson Purée (Makes more than required. Freezes well)

Combine all the ingredients in a pan and cook until soft, about 10-15 minutes. Blend until smooth, then pass through a fine sieve.

For The Duck Jus

Roast the carcass (180°C fan) in an ovenproof pan for 20 minutes. Place the pan on the stove top and add the shallot, garlic and thyme to the pan. *Deglaze* the pan with the wine and stock. Reduce until silky. When the jus lightly covers the back of a spoon, pass through a fine sieve. Add the orange segments to heat through.

For The Thyme Oil

Blanch the thyme in salted, boiling water, then dry well. Pick off the leaves and blitz with the oil. Pass through a fine sieve.

For The Kale

Reserve some kale for the garnish and *blanch* the remainder in salted, boiling water for 2 minutes. Drain well and finish with the butter.

For The Crispy Kale Garnish

Deep fry the reserved kale at 180°C for 10-15 seconds. Drain and pat dry.

To Serve

Serve as pictured.

LEMON TART, LYTH VALLEY DAMSON SORBET

SERVES 6-8

🍷 *Château Briatte de Sauternes*
(France)

Cherish your yesterdays
Dream your tomorrows
Live for today!

Ingredients

Pastry Tart Case

150g unsalted cold butter (diced)
300g plain flour (sieved)
2 large free-range eggs
salt (pinch of)
2 tbsp icing sugar
1 egg yolk (beaten)

Lemon Filling

9 large free-range eggs
400g caster sugar
5 lemons (juice of, zest of 2)
250ml double cream
2 tbsp icing sugar

Damson Sorbet

1kg damsons (stones removed)
425ml water
125g sugar

15cm loose-bottomed tart case (greased)

Method

For The Pastry Tart Case

Rub the butter into the sieved flour, then add the whole eggs, salt and icing sugar to form a dough. Add a little water if the mix is too dry. Wrap the dough in cling film and chill in the fridge for 1 hour.

Preheat the oven to 170°C (fan).

Roll the pastry to fit the prepared tart case. Line the base with baking parchment, top with baking beans and blind bake for 12 minutes. Remove the beans and paper and prick the base with a fork. Brush with beaten egg yolk to seal.

For The Lemon Filling

Turn the oven down to 120°C (fan).

Whisk the eggs, caster sugar and zest together. Stir in the cream, add the juice of 5 lemons, then pass through a fine sieve. Place the warm pastry case onto the oven shelf, pour in the cold lemon filling and bake for 25 minutes. When cool, dust the icing sugar over the top with a fine sieve. Serve at room temperature.

> **Chef's Tip**
>
> Always add the cold mix to a hot pastry case as this seals the case. If possible, fill the pastry case whilst it is in the oven to help stop spillage.

For The Damson Sorbet (Prepare ahead)

Combine the damsons, water and sugar in a pan. Boil until soft, taste and add more sugar if needed. Churn in an ice cream machine. Freeze until ready to serve.

To Serve

Serve as pictured, with the sorbet on a shortbread crumb (optional).

226
THE SUN INN

6 Market Street, Kirkby Lonsdale, Cumbria, LA6 2AU

015242 71965
www.sun-inn.info Twitter: @suninnkirkbylon Facebook: Sun Inn Bar, Restaurant & Rooms

Nestled between two national parks, The Lake District and The Yorkshire Dales, the quaint market town of Kirkby Lonsdale is home to The Sun Inn.

The 17th Century inn is set above the River Lune and a stone's throw away from 'Ruskin's View', painted by Turner and a sight dubbed by John Ruskin as "the fairest in England and therefore the world".

Led by owners Iain and Jenny Black, The Sun Inn offers a cosy bar with warm interiors, with wooden floors, exposed stone walls and log burners. The stylish restaurant reflects the traditional English countryside and the 11 contemporary rooms create a homely feel for guests.

The restaurant boasts 2 AA Rosettes and serves local seasonal ingredients combined with modern flavours to create a fine dining experience which exceeds the expectations of a traditional inn. And what makes The Sun Inn a unique fine dining experience is that it is dog-friendly, not just in the bar but in some areas of the restaurant too.

The Sun Inn at Kirkby Lonsdale can accommodate your needs with boutique hotel rooms, award-winning breakfasts and evening meals and a warm, personal service.

ORKNEY SCALLOP, LAKELAND PANCETTA, ASPARAGUS, PEAS

SERVES 4

🍷 *Cooper's Barrel Marlborough Sauvignon Blanc (New Zealand)*
Herbaceous notes marry well with the asparagus and the acidity cuts perfectly through the rich scallops.

Ingredients

4 Orkney scallops
12 asparagus stems
100g Lakeland pancetta (trimmed of fat, diced into 1cm cubes)
100g fresh peas (podded, *blanched*)
2 tbsp rapeseed oil
1 lemon (juice of)
25g butter

Garnish

Maldon sea salt
horseradish shoots and pea shoots

4 deep sided scallop shells (cleaned)

Chef's Tip

Be careful not to add the butter to the scallops too soon. You don't want to slow down the cooking time and, if the pan is too hot, the butter will burn and taint the flavour of the dish.

Method

For The Scallops

Using an oyster shucking knife, place it at the hinge of the scallop and prize it open slightly.

Turn the scallop over and run a flexible fish filleting knife over the flat side of the shell to release the scallop. Open the shell fully. Use a spoon to release the scallop from the bottom shell.

Pull off the frill, the black stomach sack and any other pieces that are around the meat of the scallop and discard, leaving just the white flesh and any coral. Rinse the scallop thoroughly in cold water.

Preheat the oven to 100°C.

Place the coral (orange roe) on baking parchment and bake for 25 minutes, or until dried. Blend the coral to a fine powder; this is going to be used to season the scallop.

For The Asparagus

Individually snap off the ends of the asparagus - where the asparagus naturally breaks is good.

Cut the tops off the spears about 5cm from the top, then *blanch* in boiling water for 30 seconds. Refresh in cold water. Finely slice the remaining part of the asparagus and set aside in a bowl.

To Cook The Scallops And Finish

Heat a large, flat frying pan and add the oil. Add the pancetta to the pan and cook for 2 minutes or until golden all over. Remove from the pan and set aside.

In the same pan add a little more oil if needed and place the scallops at 12, 3, 6 and 9 o'clock. This will help you turn them in the correct order. Cook until one side is a caramelised golden colour, approximately 1 minute.

Turn the heat down to low and turn the scallops in the same order you put them in. Add the lemon juice and butter and, while basting, cook for a further 20-30 seconds.

Remove from the pan and place on a tray, season with a little sea salt and the coral powder. Leave to rest somewhere warm.

Add the diced pancetta, peas, the sliced asparagus and tips back to the pan and warm through. Once warm, remove from the pan and set on kitchen paper to drain some of the liquid off.

To Serve

Arrange a small pile of Maldon salt onto the centre of the plate and sit the shell on top. This will help hold it in place. Place a scallop in each shell, adding all the other elements around the scallop. Garnish with the horseradish and pea shoots.

LOIN & BELLY OF SPRING LAMB

SERVES 4

🍷 *Torre dei Vescovi Pinot Nero (Italy)*
Light enough to allow the flavour of the lamb to shine through and the subtle spice works well with the dish.

Ingredients

Lamb

1 lamb belly (cut into 4 ribs, bones scraped, cleaned)
1 loin of lamb (trimmed, cut into 4 portions)

Salt Brine

100ml water, ½ lemon (juice of)
1 sprig rosemary, 1 sprig thyme
10 black peppercorns, 10 juniper berries
75g honey, 10g Maldon sea salt

Lamb Rub

½ tsp onion granules
½ tsp garlic powder, 1 lemon (zest of)

Lamb Sauce

2 carrots (roughly chopped)
1 leek (roughly chopped)
1 onion (roughly chopped)
2 sticks celery (roughly chopped)
3 tomatoes (roughly chopped)
2 sprigs rosemary, 2 sprigs thyme
4 cloves garlic, 200g lamb neck
200ml white wine, 400ml water
50g redcurrant jelly

Aubergine Jam

2 aubergines (cut into 2cm dice)
salt (to sprinkle)
2 red peppers (diced)
2 yellow peppers (diced)
1 white onion (chopped)
4 cloves garlic (minced)
oil (drizzle of)
2 tsp Chinese five spice
200g caster sugar
200ml water, 1 btl passata

To Serve

500g wild garlic (plus flowers)
butter (knob of), salt (pinch of)
diced feta and pesto (blended)

Method

For The Salt Brine (Prepare ahead)

Bring all the ingredients, except the salt, to the boil, then stir in the salt and leave to cool.

Soak the ribs in the cold brine for 4 hours and the loin for 1 hour.

For The Lamb Ribs (Prepare ahead)

Pat the ribs dry, then vac pack individually and cook in a water bath for 8 hours at 78°C. Chill quickly in ice water. Alternatively, braise in the oven at 120°C for about 5 hours. Set aside.

For The Lamb Sauce (Prepare ahead)

Brown the vegetables, herbs, garlic and lamb neck in a large, heavy-based pan. *Deglaze* with white wine. Add the water and redcurrant jelly, turn to a low heat and reduce by half, then strain.

For The Aubergine Jam (Prepare ahead)

Generously sprinkle the aubergine on a flat tray with salt and leave for 1 hour. Rinse well, then pat dry.

Sweat the peppers, onion and garlic in a pan on a low heat with a little oil and the 5 spice.

In a separate pan, fry the aubergines in oil until slightly crispy, then drain on kitchen paper.

Add the aubergines, sugar, water and passata to the pepper mix. Cook on a low heat for almost 2 hours, stirring every 20 minutes. Cool and refrigerate.

For The Lamb Loin

Dry the loin portions with kitchen paper, then coat with the lamb rub. Roll in cling film to a cylinder shape and tie both ends. Place into vac pack pouches and cook in a water bath for 15 minutes at 55°C. Alternatively, poach gently (50-60°C) for 10 minutes.

Remove from the cling film and colour in a hot pan with oil until golden. Leave to rest for at least 5 minutes.

To Serve

Preheat the oven to 160°C.

Place the cooked lamb ribs in an ovenproof dish with the lamb sauce and roast for 35-45 minutes, until it becomes slightly sticky.

Warm the aubergine jam and spoon a small *quenelle* of jam onto the plate. Slice the lamb loin into 2 pieces and place 1 rib of lamb onto a loin.

Slightly wilt the wild garlic in butter, season, then arrange around the plate. Use a little sauce from the ribs to dress the plate. Garnish with garlic flowers.

Chef's Tip

If you aren't confident preparing the belly, ask your local butcher to do this for you. You will need 4 individual portions kept on the bone.

CHOCOLATE, CHERRIES, PEANUT, BALSAMIC

SERVES 4

Late Harvest Garnacha (Spain)
Full of jammy, dark fruit on the nose and nutty notes on the palate.

Ingredients

Cherry Sorbet

150g Les Vergers Boiron Morello cherry purée
75g caster sugar
15g glucose

Base

60g flour
60g unsalted butter
30g caster sugar
60g salted peanuts (blended to a fine powder)

Chocolate Marquise

120g dark chocolate 70%
40g egg yolks
1 large egg
50g honey
120ml whipping cream
4g Maldon sea salt

Cherry And Balsamic Jelly

50ml cherry juice
25ml kirsch
10ml balsamic vinegar
1 leaf gelatine

To Serve

15g shortbread crumb (reserved from the base)
20 Griottines cherries
micro lemon balm

4 x 8cm baking rings (greased)

Chef's Tip

If you don't own an ice cream machine you can put the sorbet in the freezer and whisk thoroughly every 20 minutes until the right consistency is achieved.

Method

For The Cherry Sorbet

Heat all the ingredients together in a pan and bring to the boil. Strain through a fine sieve and leave to cool fully before churning in an ice cream machine for about 1 hour. Freeze until needed.

For The Base

Preheat the oven to 180°C.

Crumb together the flour, sugar and 40g of the butter and bake on a flat tray until golden brown, about 12 minutes.

Remove from the oven and break down the shortbread to a crumb. Put 15g of the crumb to one side to sit the sorbet on later.

Melt the remaining butter and combine thoroughly with the remaining shortbread crumb and powdered peanuts.

Place the prepared rings on a flat tray lined with baking parchment. Add the base to the rings, a tablespoon at a time and compress with a rolling pin to a ½cm depth. Place in the fridge to set.

For The Chocolate Marquise

Melt the chocolate in a *bain-marie*.

Whip the yolks in a food mixer or with an electric whisk until pale and fluffy. Add the whole egg and whisk until well incorporated.

Bring the honey to a simmer in a pan and slowly add to the egg mixture while whisking on a medium speed. Once mixed, leave to one side.

Whisk the cream to soft peaks in a separate bowl, then stir through the melted chocolate.

Fold together the egg mixture, chocolate cream and salt.

When the bases have set, fill the rings with the marquise mix, leaving 3mm of space to pour the jelly on later. Set in the fridge for 1 hour.

For The Cherry And Balsamic Jelly

Add all the ingredients cold to a pan and leave for 10 minutes to allow the gelatine to bloom. Bring to the boil slowly, stirring all the time.

Pass the jelly through a fine sieve into a jug and leave at room temperature until the marquise has set. Once set, pour a thin layer of jelly on top before returning to the fridge for about 20 minutes.

To Serve

Place each dessert onto a plate and, with a blow torch, lightly heat the ring being careful not to catch the jelly on top. The rings will release allowing you to slowly lift them off.

Arrange a little of the reserved crumb to the side and sit the sorbet on top. Garnish with the cherries and micro lemon balm. Serve immediately.

236
TWELVE
RESTAURANT

Marsh Mill Village, Thornton Cleveleys, Lancashire, FY5 4JZ

01253 82 12 12
www.twelve-restaurant.co.uk Twitter: @twelvethornton Facebook: @twelvethornton

Stylish and contemporary with a modern British menu, Twelve Restaurant is located on the Lancashire coast at Marsh Mill Village under the historic 1794 windmill in Thornton Cleveleys. Twelve has an urban, industrial, ultra-modern look, with exposed air ducts, brick walls, wooden and slate flooring and designer furniture.

Twelve is owned and has been operated since 2000 by husband and wife team, Paul Moss and Caroline Upton who are self-confessed foodies. They have a reputation for creativity and culinary excellence, combined with great warmth and geniality and are passionate about dining and hospitality. Twelve's bold and innovative cooking using regionally sourced seasonal produce has brought it critical acclaim and numerous national awards. Twelve was awarded a Michelin Bib Gourmand in 2005 and 2 AA Rosettes in 2007, which it has proudly retained annually since then. The restaurant has grown over the years with the outside catering arm of the business now providing its food at iconic venues across Lancashire.

"We owe much to our team who have travelled with us on our journey over the years. The chefs are passionate about developing and experimenting to create exquisite food with exceptional attention to detail, with the front of house team giving a level of service to exceed expectations, although always relaxed." said Caroline Upton.

Head chef Graham Floyd works closely with his team to create an experience which showcases the best of Lancashire produce in the height of its season. Working with regional producers and suppliers he delivers stimulating, skilful modern cookery with clarity and cleanness of flavours.

Twelve's ethos remains the same as when the doors opened in 2000. The aim is always to deliver a flawless organisation, spectacular design, delicious food and drink delivered by a highly personable and professional staff.

HERITAGE TOMATO & MOZZARELLA SALAD, CHARRED CUCUMBER, CANDIED HAZELNUTS

SERVES 4

Basil Infused G&T - Batch Premium Gin muddled with fresh basil, strain, pour over crushed ice, top with Fentimans tonic. Garnish with fresh basil.

Ingredients

500g mixed heritage English tomatoes
1 buffalo mozzarella

Tomato Chutney

1 large onion (finely diced)
50ml white wine vinegar
1 tsp ground ginger
1 tsp ground cinnamon
1 tsp fennel seeds
300g ripe salad tomatoes (roughly chopped)
100g dates (chopped, soaked)
50g granulated sugar

Balsamic Glaze

250ml balsamic vinegar
75g granulated sugar
1 stick cinnamon
2 star anise
3 pink peppercorns

Charred Cucumber

1 English cucumber (peeled)
25ml gin (your choice, ours is Batch Premium Gin distilled in Burnley)

Candied Hazelnuts

100g hazelnuts
100g granulated sugar

Garnish

rye bread croutons
edible flowers or herbs
rapeseed oil (drizzle of)
Maldon salt (to season)

Method

For The Tomato Chutney

Place the onion in a heavy-based saucepan with the vinegar and reduce by half. Add the spices, aromats and tomatoes to the pan and simmer for 20-30 minutes until the tomatoes are cooked through. Add the dates and sugar, cook for a further 2 minutes. Set aside to cool.

For The Balsamic Glaze

Place all the ingredients into a heavy-based saucepan and reduce until thick and sticky. This should take 15-20 minutes at a steady simmer, then cool.

For The Charred Cucumber

Slice the cucumber into 1cm thick slices, place into a vac pack bag with the gin and seal tight using a vacuum chamber. Leave for 10 minutes. Drain onto a rack, then char with a blow torch.

> **Chef's Tip**
>
> Soak the cucumber in your chosen gin for 30 minutes if you do not have access to a vacuum chamber.

For The Candied Hazelnuts

Preheat the oven to 180°C.

Roast the hazelnuts for 10-25 minutes until the skins begin to fall off. Roll them in a clean tea towel to remove all the skin. Caramelise the sugar in a saucepan and fold in the hazelnuts. Leave to cool on a tray, then break up the candied hazelnuts.

To Serve

Slice the heritage tomatoes into random bite size wedges and slices. Place onto the plate with the torched cucumber slices and tomato chutney. Tear up the buffalo mozzarella and divide evenly between the plates, then crumble the candied hazelnuts over the salad. Season with rapeseed oil, balsamic glaze and Maldon salt before placing on the rye bread croutons and edible flowers.

BEEF CHEEK COOKED IN HAY, PICKLED BEETROOT, ONIONS, CREAMED POTATO

SERVES 4

Château Haut-Monplaisir Tradition, Cahors
(France)

Ingredients

Beef Cheek
2 raw beef cheeks (trimmed)
100g clean eating hay
200ml pomace oil (plus extra for frying)
25g salted butter
6 sprigs thyme, 3 cloves garlic
Maldon salt (to season)

Onion Purée
6 white onions (sliced)
100ml pomace oil
100ml water
25g granulated sugar
table salt (to season)

Creamed Potato
1kg Maris Piper potatoes (peeled)
salt (pinch of), 100ml whole milk
100ml double cream, 50g salted butter

Red Wine Jus
100ml pomace oil
1 shallot (thinly sliced)
1 carrot (thinly sliced)
1 leek (thinly sliced)
1 stick celery (thinly sliced)
1 clove garlic (thinly sliced)
1 thyme sprig, 1 rosemary sprig
1 bay leaf, 500ml red wine
500ml reduced veal stock

Pickled Beetroot
3 raw red beetroot (peeled)
100g granulated sugar
25ml white wine vinegar
100ml water, 2 sprigs thyme

Braised Onion Skins
4 baby onions (whole, skin on)
100ml fresh chicken stock
25ml pomace oil

Method

For The Beef Cheek (Prepare ahead)
Place the beef cheeks into individual *sous vide* bags with the hay and pomace oil, then seal tightly in a vacuum chamber. Place into a water bath set at 82°C for 8 hours, then remove and chill. This can be made in advance and be stored in the fridge for 2-3 days.

Chef's Tip

If you do not have access to a water bath, braise the beef cheek in beef stock and a vegetable *mirepoix* at 110°C for 4 hours.

For The Onion Purée
Sauté the onions with the pomace oil in a heavy-based pan until golden. Add the water and sugar and cook out until the onions are soft. Blend in a food blender until smooth. Season and pass the purée through a fine sieve.

For The Creamed Potato
Chop the potatoes into even-sized pieces and boil with salt until soft. Drain and return to the dry pan over a medium heat, stirring to avoid them sticking. Pass the potatoes through a *chinois*, season with salt, milk, cream and butter. Transfer to a piping bag and keep warm.

For The Red Wine Jus
Place a medium pan onto a high heat and add the pomace oil. As soon as the pan begins to smoke add the vegetables and garlic. Cook until golden brown in colour, then add the herbs and red wine. Turn the heat down and simmer, reduce the liquid down to a syrup (50ml). Add the veal stock and simmer for a further 5 minutes, then pass through a fine sieve.

For The Beetroot
Slice the beetroot thinly on a mandoline. Bring the sugar, vinegar, water and thyme to the boil and simmer for 3 minutes. Cool slightly, then pour over the sliced beets. Leave for 1 hour to pickle. Drain on kitchen towel before serving.

For The Braised Onion Skins
Simmer the onions in the stock for 20-30 minutes until soft. Slice the onions in half, then char in a little pomace oil, flat-side down, in a hot pan. Peel and set aside.

To Serve
Slice each beef cheek in half and seal in a frying pan with the pomace oil, butter, thyme and garlic. Baste the cheeks in the pan for 2-3 minutes on either side, then season and drain on kitchen towel. Serve as pictured.

DARK CHOCOLATE PAVE, STRAWBERRY SORBET, LANCASHIRE STRAWBERRIES

SERVES 4

 Pineau Des Charentes Rouge 5 Years Old, Château de Beaulon (France)

Ingredients

Chocolate Sponge

7 medium whole eggs
200g caster sugar
100g plain flour
100g cocoa powder

Chocolate Pavé

400g dark chocolate 55%
4 egg yolks
25g caster sugar
450ml double cream

Chocolate Glaze

100ml water
100ml double cream
100g caster sugar
50g cocoa powder
3 leaves gelatine (soaked in cold water)

Strawberry Sorbet

200g caster sugar
200ml water
500ml fresh strawberry purée

To Serve

250g fresh UK strawberries
100ml fresh strawberry purée (to garnish)
red vein sorrel (to garnish)

4 x 7cm metal ring moulds

Method

For The Chocolate Sponge

Preheat the oven to 165°C.

Whisk the whole eggs and caster sugar until light and fluffy. Sift the cocoa powder and flour into the egg mix and fold through thoroughly. Spread the mixture out onto a baking tray lined with baking paper, the mix should be evenly spread about 3mm thick. Bake in the oven for 5-7 minutes. Cool on a wire rack, then cut out your desired shape to fit your moulds.

For The Chocolate Pavé

Melt the chocolate in a *bain-marie*. Whisk the egg yolks and sugar together until light and fluffy. Whip half of the double cream to a soft peak. Take the melted chocolate off the heat and add the egg mixture to it, then fold in the whipped cream. Finally, fold in the remaining double cream until the mixture is glossy. Pour the mixture over the sponge base into the moulds and leave to set in the fridge for 1 hour. Pop the pavé out of the metal rings onto a wire rack.

For The Chocolate Glaze

Mix all the ingredients, apart from the gelatine, in a saucepan and gently bring to the boil. Whisk in the drained gelatine, then pass through a fine sieve. Pour on top of the pavé, making sure to cover generously. All the excess will fall through the wire rack. Set in the fridge for 10 minutes, then remove from the wire rack and store in the fridge for up to 2 days.

For The Strawberry Sorbet (Prepare ahead)

Bring the sugar and water to the boil in a saucepan. Once the sugar has dissolved, add the strawberry purée and leave to cool. Churn in an ice cream machine. Store in the freezer for up to 4 weeks.

To Serve

Prepare and rinse the strawberries. Arrange 3 to 4 of them on each plate with some of the fresh strawberry purée and add a *quenelle* of the sorbet. Carefully place the pavé on the plate and finally finish with red vein sorrel.

Chef's Tip

Use a blow torch to heat the ring mould for 3 seconds and the pavé should pop straight out. Use a crumb to secure the sorbet to the plate, such as caramelised white chocolate.

FINE FOOD & VEGETABLES

LUNYA
18-20 College Lane, Liverpool, L1 3DS T: 0151 706 9770
Barton Arcade, Deansgate, Manchester, M3 2BB
T: 0161 413 3317
www.lunya.co.uk
The wines and specialist meats and spices used in Lunya's recipes, pages 190-195, are available in store, or online.

OLIVER KAY PRODUCE
Produce House, Britannia Way, Bolton, BL2 2HH
T: 08448 479 790 www.oliverkayproduce.co.uk
Fruit and vegetable suppliers and speciality foods.

R. NOONE & SON
Southside, Bredbury Park Way, Stockport, SK6 2SP
T: 0161 406 8633 www.rnooneandson.co.uk
Wholesale fruit and vegetable merchant.

UDALE SPECIALITY FOODS
1 Schola Green Lane, Morecambe, LA4 5QT
T: 01524 411611 www.udale.com
A family-owned business run by brothers, Ian and Neil Udale, the company was founded by their great grandfather in 1905. Award-winners at the North West Fine Foods' Awards since 2002. Awards included: Best Lamb, Best Beef, Best Pork, Venison Sausage, Pork and Chutney Pie, and for those with a sweet tooth, the luxury vanilla pod ice cream.

WELLOCKS
4 Pendleside, Lomeshaye Business Village,
Lancashire, BB9 6SH
T: 08444 993 444 www.wellocks.co.uk
Founded in 1961, suppliers of quality vegetables, fruit and a range of dairy and bakery products mainly sourced from local producers and farms.

DAIRY

DUNHAM MASSEY FARM ICE CREAM
Ash Farm, Dunham Massey, Altrincham, Cheshire, WA14 5SG
T: 0161 928 1230
A mother and daughter partnership producing 20 flavours of ice cream, all handmade with double cream and whole milk.

GORNALL'S DAIRY FOODS
Bushell's Farm, Goosnargh, Preston, PR3 2BJ
T: 01772 865763 www.gornallsdairyfoods.co.uk
A third generation family business established in 1910, offering a fast, friendly and reliable dairy food delivery service.

PROCTORS CHEESE LTD
The Cheese Warehouse, Saunders Raikem Chipping,
Nr Preston, Lancashire, PR3 2QR
T: 0199 561 626 www.procterscheeses.co.uk
The Proctor family has been making cheese in the picturesque village of Chipping since the 1930s and the company is now run by the fourth generation of Proctors. The local farms have lush pastures which ensures the production of excellent milk for cheese making.

247 LARDER

WINE

FRANK STAINTON WINE MERCHANTS
1 Station Road, Kendal, Cumbria, LA9 6BT
www.stainton-wines.co.uk
Importers and sellers of quality wines.

FISH

NEVES OF FLEETWOOD
19 Copse Road, Fleetwood, Lancashire, FY7 6RP
T: 01253 774 100 www.nevefleetwood.co.uk
Neve Fleetwood for wholesale fish and shellfish supplies.

THE EASY FISH COMPANY
Heaton Moor, Stockport, SK4 4HY
T: 0161 442 0823 www.theeasyfishco.com
An independent family-run business with 120 years' experience in the fish trade.

MEAT

BREDBURY CATERING BUTCHERS
Phoenix Court, Hammond Avenue, Stockport, SK4 1PQ
T: 0161 476 3237
Specialist catering butchers providing meat to hotels, public houses, restaurants, nursing homes, colleges and the general public.

CARTMEL VALLEY GAME SUPPLIES & SMOKEHOUSE
High Bankside, Cark-In-Cartmel, Grange-Over-Sands, Cumbria, LA11 7NR
T: 01539 536 413
www.cartmelvalleygamesupplies.com
Cartmel Valley Game nestles in the picturesque historical Cartmel Valley, where Jonathan and Susan run their successful game business from their beautiful Lake District home. They work closely with their team of highly qualified and dedicated staff, supplying the best quality gourmet game and smoked products to top class establishments.

HAMPTON FARM SHOP
Malpas, Cheshire, SY14 8JQ
T: 01948 820 528 www.hamptonfarmshop.co.uk
Farm shop supplying meats, poultry and local game.

J & S GOOSNARGH LTD
Johnson & Swarbrick, Swainson House Farm, Goosnargh, Preston, Lancashire, PR3 2JU
T: 01772 865 251 www.jandsgoosnargh.co.uk
Situated on the edge of the Ribble Valley, in the picturesque village of Goosnargh, Johnson & Swarbrick have been producing fine poultry products for the past three decades.

BAKERS

LOVINGLY ARTISAN BAKERY
Crook Road, Kendal, Cumbria, LA8 8LX
T: 01539 736664 www.lovinglyartisan.com
Specialist sourdough bakery.

AL DENTE
Al dente describes vegetables that are cooked to the 'tender crisp' phase - still offering resistance to the bite, but cooked through. Al dente can also describe cooked pasta which is firm but not hard.

BAIN-MARIE
A pan or other container of hot water with a bowl placed on top of it. This allows the steam from the water to heat the bowl so ingredients can be gently heated or melted.

BEURRE NOISETTE
Unsalted butter is melted over a low heat until it begins to caramelise and brown. When it turns a nutty colour, it should be removed from the heat to stop it burning. Can be used as a base for butter sauces or added to cakes and batters.

BLANCH
Boiling an ingredient before removing it and plunging it in ice cold water in order to stop the cooking process.

BRUNOISE
A type of culinary cut in which food is diced into 3.175mm cubes. The formal-looking little squares add colour and elegance to dishes.

CARTOUCHE
A piece of greaseproof paper that covers the surface of a stew, soup, stock or sauce to reduce evaporation.

CHINOIS
A conical sieve with an extremely fine mesh. It is used to strain custards, purées, soups and sauces, producing a very smooth texture.

CLARIFIED BUTTER
Milk fat rendered from butter to separate the milk solids and water from the butter fat.

CONFIT
A method of cooking where the meat is cooked and submerged in a liquid to add flavour. Often this liquid is rendered fat. Confit can also apply to fruits - fruit confits are cooked and preserved in sugar, the result is like candied fruits.

DEGLAZE
To make a gravy or sauce by adding liquid to the cooking juices and food particles in a pan in which meat or other ingredients have been cooked.

EMULSION/EMULSIFY
In the culinary arts, an emulsion is a mixture of two liquids that would ordinarily not mix together, like oil and vinegar.

FRENCH TRIMMED
To French trim, fat, meat or skin is cut away to expose a piece of bone, so that it sticks out.

It also means that any excess fat is cut off. French Trimming can be done to lamb chops and bigger cuts; it can even can be done to chicken legs or breasts.

JULIENNE
A culinary knife cut in which the vegetable is sliced into long thin strips, similar to matchsticks.

LIQUOR
The liquid that is left over from the cooking of meat or vegetables. Can be incorporated into sauces and gravy.

MIREPOIX

Finely diced combination of celery (pascal, celery or celeriac), onions and carrots. There are many regional mirepoix variations, which can sometimes be just one of these ingredients, or include additional spices creating a rich, flavoursome base to sauces or stews.

NAGE

A term for a flavoured liquid used for poaching delicate foods, typically seafood. A traditional nage is a broth flavoured with white wine, vegetables and herbs, in which seafood is poached. The liquid is then reduced and thickened with cream and/or butter.

PANE

To coat with flour, beaten egg and breadcrumbs for deep frying.

QUENELLE

A neat, three-sided oval (resembling a mini rugby ball) that is formed by gently smoothing the mixture between two dessertspoons.

RENDER/RENDERED

To melt the fat from the meat in order to clarify it.

SABAYON

Made by beating egg yolks with a liquid over simmering water until thickened and increased in volume. The liquid can be water, but Champagne or wine is often used.

SAUTE

To fry in a small amount of fat.

SHUCK

To carefully remove the shell or natural covering from something that can be eaten.

SOUS VIDE

French for 'under vacuum.' A method of cooking food sealed in airtight plastic bags in a water bath or in a temperature-controlled steam environment for longer than normal cooking times. The intention is to cook the item evenly, ensuring that the inside is properly cooked without overcooking the outside, and to retain moisture.

TEMPER

To temper eggs is to add a hot liquid to an egg mixture without cooking the eggs. Tempering is to slowly bring up the temperature of the eggs without scrambling them.

Tempering also refers to a process of heating and cooling chocolate to prepare it for dipping and enrobing. The tempering process ensures a smooth texture, a glossy shine and a pleasant 'snap' when bitten or broken.

TURN

A classic technique used in French cuisine. Vegetables are 'turned' in order to form exactly the same barrel shape and size thus ensuring even cooking while being pleasing to the eye.

ALL THE INGREDIENTS FOR YOUR RECIPE TO SUCCESS

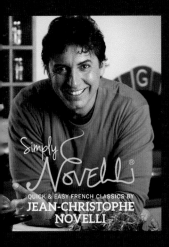

Relish is proud to have worked with more than 1500 of the UK's finest chefs to showcase their wonderful restaurants and food but there is a huge appetite for more.

Mark Greenaway and Jean Christophe Novelli are just two of the industry's leading lights who worked with our small, professional and dedicated team to produce their own beautiful books - stamped with their personality and signature dishes.

We are delighted and proud to share with you the news that Mark's book Perceptions was named the world's best chef cookbook at the Gourmand World Cookbook Awards 2017. It is an amazing accolade and testament to Mark's passion for the art and the wonderful natural larder he works with. Perceptions is an outstanding example of how, as an independent publisher, we are able to focus on you, your restaurant and your region to showcase culinary excellence to our readers who are always hungry to try out new dishes.

Owning this book is just for starters, reading it is the main course. Why not go for dessert and let us help you create a bespoke publication of your own to share with your loyal customers and attract new fans along the way? You will be on the shelves alongside our fantastic portfolio of beautifully illustrated guides, which are stocked nationally in Waterstones, Harvey Nichols, in each featured restaurant, in leading independent stores and online globally. You could be the next published chef to join the world's elite

Relish has a small, friendly, professional team, with experience in publishing, print management, editing, proofing, photography, design and artwork, sales distribution and marketing. We ensure a personal approach, working exceptionally hard to develop a great product which reflects each chef's talent and passion.

Duncan and Teresa Peters established the company in 2009, with a vision of building a niche publishing house for food lovers. The success of Relish Publications is reflected in the fact that we are the UK's leading regional recipe book publisher.

To book a personal consultation with our friendly, dedicated team contact our head office on 01670 571 635.

"Relish books are full of enjoyable recipes and ideas for making the most of the edible treasures we have on our doorstep; both places to eat them and new, exciting ways to cook them."

Angela Hartnett, MBE

"The Relish cookbook offers the home cook some great inspiration to make the most of these wonderful ingredients in season."

Tom Kitchin

"With mouthwatering, easy to follow recipes and beautiful photography, this book is a must have for any foodie, from professional chef to the inspired home cook."

Michael Caines MBE

"The North East and Yorkshire has an amazing food and drink scene with a fantastic array of produce and restaurants - available on your doorstep. Relish gives you a taste of what we all have to offer through the pages of this superb book."

Kenny Atkinson

"Relish Midlands is a fantastic recipe book that brings together so many of the talented chefs and quality restaurants in the area. It gives you a taste of what our exciting region has to offer as well as the encouragement to try some new recipes."

Adam Stokes

"Relish Wales is a fabulous way to showcase some of our beautiful country's fabulous eateries and to be able to share our food with a wider audience."

Stephen Terry

AVAILABLE TO BUY IN OUR FEATURED RESTAURANTS & IN ALL GOOD BOOKSHOPS

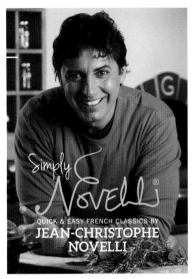

Simply *Novelli*®

QUICK & EASY FRENCH CLASSICS BY
JEAN-CHRISTOPHE NOVELLI

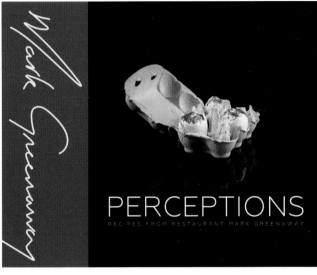

Mark Greenaway

PERCEPTIONS
RECIPES FROM RESTAURANT MARK GREENAWAY

Relish
NORTH WEST
Original recipes from the region's
finest chefs and restaurants.
Introduction by Paul Heathcote, MBE.

Relish
SOUTH EAST
Original recipes from the region's
finest chefs and restaurants.
Introduction by Angela Hartnett, MBE.

Relish
SCOTLAND
THIRD HELPING
Original recipes from the region's finest chefs
and restaurants. Featuring the Michelin starred
chefs of Scotland.

Relish
NORTH EAST & YORKSHIRE
SECOND HELPING
Original recipes from the North East and Yorkshire's finest chefs and restaurants. Introduction by Kenny Atkinson.

Relish
SOUTH WEST
Original recipes from the South West's finest chefs and restaurants. Introduction by Michael Caines MBE.

Relish
WALES
SECOND HELPING
Original recipes from the region's finest chefs and restaurants. Introduction by James Sommerin.

THIRD EDITION

Relish
WALES
Original recipes from the region's finest chefs and restaurants. Introduction by chef Will Holland.

Relish
SOUTH WEST
SECOND HELPING
Original recipes from the South West's finest chefs and restaurants. Introduction by chef Nathan Outlaw.

Relish
MIDLANDS
SECOND HELPING
Original recipes from the region's finest chefs and restaurants. Introduction by Adam Stokes.

254
HINTS & TIPS

HOW TO MAKE ICE CREAM WITHOUT A MACHINE

Although relatively inexpensive these days, not everyone has access to an ice cream machine. That's no reason not to follow some of these delicious recipes found in the Relish North West book. Although more time consuming than a machine, excellent results can be obtained by following this simple method.

Follow the recipe right up until it tells you to churn in the machine, including any chilling time in the fridge.

Take your mixture from the fridge and stir with a rubber spatula. Transfer it to a suitable plastic container with a lid. There should be at least 2cm space at the top to allow the mixture to expand when freezing. Cover and place in the freezer for two hours.

Remove from the freezer and beat with a hand mixer, still in the container, to break up the ice crystals that are beginning to form. Cover and return to the freezer for a further 2 hours. (If you don't have a hand mixer then you may use a fork and some 'elbow grease' to break up the crystals).

Remove from the freezer and beat again with the hand mixer. The ice cream should be thickening up nicely at this point but too soft to scoop. Return it to the freezer for an additional hour. Beat again. If your ice cream is still not thickened sufficiently, repeat this process again after another hour. When the ice cream has thickened properly, stir in any add-ins at this point (honeycomb, nuts...). Do not beat with the hand mixer after the add-ins have been mixed in.

Place the tightly sealed container in the freezer and allow the ice cream to freeze until firm. The ice cream should be removed from the freezer 15-20 minutes before you wish to eat it. This will make scooping easier.

This method will also work for sorbets. Sometimes sorbets may go a bit 'icy' or 'crumbly' if left for too long in the freezer. This can be rectified by blitzing in a food processor just before serving.

Peanut Butter Semifreddo, Banana Ice Cream - **Page 164**

HOW TO MAKE A SUGAR STOCK SYRUP

This makes about 750ml sugar stock. It can be stored in a sterilised jar in the fridge for a couple of months.

500g white sugar
500ml water

Place the sugar and water in a pan. Dissolve slowly over a very low heat. You must not allow the syrup to boil until all the sugar has dissolved, about 5 minutes. Once completely dissolved, bring to the boil, then simmer for 5 minutes.

CONVERSION CHART

COOKING TEMPERATURES

Degrees Celsius	Fahrenheit	Gas Mark
140	275	1
150	300	2
160-170	325	3
180	350	4
190	375	5
200-210	400	6
220	425	7
230	450	8
240	475	9

*Temperatures for fan-assisted ovens are, as a general rule, normally about 20°C lower than regular oven temperatures.

WEIGHT MEASUREMENT CONVERSIONS

teaspoon (5ml/5g)	$^1/_4$ oz
tablespoon (15ml/15g)	$^3/_4$ oz
0g	$^1/_2$ oz
5g	1oz
0g	2oz
5g	3oz
50g	5oz
00g	7oz
50g	9oz
50g	12oz
50g	1lb
kg	2.2lb

VOLUME MEASUREMENT CONVERSIONS

55ml	2 fl oz
150ml	$^1/_4$ pt
275ml	$^1/_2$ pt
570ml	1 pt
1 litre	$1^3/_4$ pt

Roast Sea Bass, White & Green English Asparagus, Chive Emulsion - **Page 210**